53

ways to enhance
researcher development

Edited by
Rob Daley
Kay Guccione
Steve Hutchinson

ISBN: 978-1-907076-95-4 (paperback edition)
        978-1-907076-96-1 (ePub edition)
        978-1-907076-97-8 (PDF edition)

Published under The Professional and Higher Partnership imprint
by Frontinus Ltd
Registered office: Suite 7, Lyndon House, 8 King's Court,
Willie Snaith Road, Newmarket, Suffolk, CB8 7SG, UK

Company website: pandhp.com

This edition published 2017.

Credits
Cover image: Rika Newcombe (rikanewcombe.co.uk)
Cover design and typesetting: Benn Linfield (bennlinfield.com)
Abstract: Anthony Haynes
Copy-editing: Karen Haynes
Proofreading: Will Dady
E-book conversion: CPI
Printers: TJ International and Lightning Source

Disclaimer

Frontinus Ltd has no responsibility for the persistence or accuracy of URLs for external or third-party websites referred to in this publication, and does not guarantee that any content on such websites is, or will remain, accurate or appropriate.

The material contained in this publication is provided in good faith as general guidance. The advice and strategies contained herein may not be suitable for every situation. No liability can be accepted by Frontinus Ltd for any liability, loss, risk, or damage which is incurred as a consequence, whether direct or indirect, of using or applying any of the contents of this book or the advice or guidance contained therein.

The publisher and the author make no warranties or representations with respect to the completeness or accuracy of the contents of this work and specifically disclaim all warranties, including without limitation warranties of fitness for a particular purpose. No warranty may be created or extended by sales or promotional materials.

Copyright: rights deals and permissions
To acquire rights, including translation rights, or permission to reproduce text, please contact our rights manager via info@frontinus.org.uk.

Professional and Higher Education: series information

Titles in the Professional and Higher Education series include:

53 interesting things to do in your lectures
53 interesting things to do in your seminars and tutorials
53 interesting ways of helping your students to study
53 ways to deal with large classes
53 interesting ways to communicate your research
53 interesting ways to assess your students
53 interesting ways to support online learning
53 ways to enhance researcher development

Contents

Abstract

As the result of recent changes in the research landscape, researchers are now commonly required to do more than just research. For example, they are often expected to take responsibility for post-research activities, including engagement with government, business, and the public. To meet these expectations, an array of skills is required, including communication, networking, leadership, and the management of stakeholders. The need to develop such skills in researchers presents a challenge to those responsible for their development. These include researcher developers, principal investigators, research supervisors, staff developers, careers professionals, research office staff, and research centre managers. These developers face additional demands from the need to help researchers develop their careers and employability. 53 solutions, each tested in practice, for meeting these challenges are presented here, accompanied by practical advice on their implementation and the potential pitfalls involved.

Key terms: research; researcher development; staff development; academic development; career development.

Publishers' foreword

Each book in the Professional and Higher Education series provides constructive ideas that are rooted in practice and readily applicable.

Originally designed to support teaching and learning in post-compulsory education, the series first expanded into new territory (namely, research) with 53 *interesting ways to communicate your research*. We're pleased now to introduce this latest title as a contribution to the nascent field of publications for practitioners in researcher development.

Like other books in the series, this one is designed for dipping into to find ideas that dovetail with the reader's practice. Readers can, therefore, each design their own path through the book. To facilitate navigation, the ideas in the book are grouped in ten thematic chapters, and suggestions for related ideas are listed at the end of each section.

If you enjoy this book, we hope that you might wish to explore some of the further 371 ideas currently available in the series. ☺

Anthony Haynes and Karen Haynes

Editors' preface

In recent years, the international research landscape has undergone many significant changes. These changes have resulted in a need for researchers to modify their standard practice and develop new skills and approaches to maintain their competitiveness. Across the world, researchers are being required to do much more than just research, and are now responsible for many of the elements associated with post-research activities. Many of these activities are required by research funders or by the institutions in which the researchers work. The quality of these endeavours is often assessed through national research assessment processes and counts towards the assessment outcomes that are linked to national funding schemes and other funding elements. Among these new challenges for researchers are an increasing expectation of engagement with policy makers and the public, and an increased expectation to explore commercial benefits that may accrue from their research. There is also an ever-increasing open research agenda, with a growing expectation that researchers will make their research publications available through open access and publically share their research data. Alongside this, there is now an expectation in many countries that researchers are also responsible for enhancing the economic and societal impact that their research has – and for evaluating this. These new expectations require researchers to alter their practices, to learn new skills, and to develop networks and communication channels with various research users and practitioners. In addition, the increasing numbers of larger funded projects and block funding of doctoral students require researchers to acquire new leadership and management skills.

These new and ever-changing expectations for researchers mean that the role of researcher developers is evolving to ensure that we can support our researchers to be successful in these new elements of their practice. In addition to supporting the areas mentioned above, there is an increasing expectation that researcher developers will support the career development and employability of doctoral students and early career research staff, support the career development of academic staff, and provide leadership development for principal investigators and research leaders. While in some institutions these elements may be managed in collaboration with other staff groups or units, these are not areas that we can or should ignore. Researcher developers are also increasingly finding ways to contribute to the development and implementation of institutional research strategy and policy.

Researcher development is a responsibility and activity of far more people than those occupying researcher development posts or roles. Many people across our institutions have both an interest in, and responsibility for, supporting the development of our researchers. These include principal investigators, research supervisors, staff developers, careers professionals, research office staff and research centre mangers. Principal investigators and research supervisors have a dual role in this context. They are both researchers who would benefit from developmental support, and have responsibility for supporting the development of the researchers they manage and supervise. Researcher development is very much a shared concern, with multiple actors and multiple stakeholders.

There is also much consideration and debate around the professional identity of researcher developers and a steady expansion in the trappings of such a profession. There are a growing number of national and international conferences aimed at and organised by researcher developers. There is a growth in the research around researcher development activities, with researcher developers occupying both the role of researcher and research subject in these studies. Moreover, there is an international journal dedicated to researcher development and many papers are appearing in other journals focusing on researcher development issues. The initial findings of one research project investigating the experiences and career paths of UK-based researcher developers are presented in the appendix to this book. This outlines the key findings of a 2015 survey that sought to identify the commonalities and diversity of the roles and responsibilities of UK-based researcher developers.

As the roles of researcher developers and the expectations around them expand, we felt it was timely to gather together the views and experiences of a number of experienced researcher developers. This book has been put together to provide an opportunity for researcher developers to share their expertise and approaches with others and to provide stimulation for all those involved in supporting and developing researchers. It is our hope that the various elements within these chapters will provide new ideas for researcher developers to enrich their practice and will encourage more innovative support for all our researchers.

Rob Daley, Kay Guccione and Steve Hutchinson

Chapter 1
Researcher development
in context

1

1 Developmental needs analysis: if a workshop is the answer – what's the question?

Do either of these scenarios sound familiar?

The participant declaration of 'I thought I'd come along to the workshop today as "it" may come in useful some time.'

Or, a departmental request of 'We need a workshop on [for example] how to boil an egg' and we reply with 'Yes, of course!' without asking why there is a need to learn how to boil an egg – and if there is, whether a workshop is the best way to learn how to do so.

Are either of the above based on an actual *need* for development? How do we know? As researcher developers we can make ourselves very busy sheep-dipping researchers through workshops and spinning on the hamster wheel of programme planning because we're paid to do it or expected to as a service department, while achieving very little in real terms.

This is a fundamental issue for us as researcher developers, for if we aren't addressing a real need – what's the point? In order to do this, we need to need to engage with our stakeholders with the right question.

Individual researchers

We can help *individual researchers* think about what they really need rather than want by *challenging* them to answer the following themselves:

- Where do I want to get to?
- What do I want the outcome to be? What's the benefit to me?
- What do I need to be able to do to achieve the outcome?
- What development activities will help me?

When planning precisely what they need to do:

- How will the activity help me achieve research outputs and impact?
- Will the activity provide evidence that will enhance my CV?
- Will the activity allow me to develop myself through practice, feedback and feedforward?

We should focus on creating learning and development activity that researchers respond to because it benefits and interests them and because it helps them to grow.

Supervisors, research groups and departments

How do we help supervisors, research groups and departments really think about what is needed? If we work in partnership with them to co-design, develop and deliver researcher development, the activity will be specific, focused and deliver the results they want. Here are some key questions to ask:

- Where are you now in terms of the identified need/issue?
- Where would you like to be?
- What development activity will result in something of tangible value for the individuals and the organisation?
- What development activity will help in building a research community?

By asking the right questions and probing what lies behind the answers, we can make a real difference, using our expertise in developing good quality learning.

Research institutions

Last (but definitely not least!), how do we help institutions really think about what is needed? We should be the institution's critical friend – being willing to question and support the institution to undertake change in response to current and future challenges in the research landscape. In order to do this we need to: utilise our knowledge and understanding of institutional, national and international developments in policy; identify trends in the employment of researchers; cultivate close links with researcher developers; and network with organisations, networks and funding bodies.

Most importantly, researcher developers need to engage with research and scholarship so that we can make evidence-based recommendations for enhancement of programmes and activities. By asking the right research questions we will be able to address researcher needs at all levels – individual, research group, departments and faculties, and institution – and not just spin the hamster wheel for another academic year.

Heather Sears

Complementary ideas include **4** and **11**.

2 Mapping the culture: listening to the researcher voice

The components of researcher development have evolved significantly in recent years and so researcher developers must be prepared to look at their roles through a much wider lens than that of event providers. The role affords an amazing opportunity for both contributing to and driving organisational change. One way in which to achieve this is to really canvass and utilise the researcher voice.

Conversation as a tool

Focused conversations are a method to successfully canvass the researcher voice in a way that is meaningful and tailored to the institution. Rather than using formulaic engagement surveys, there is significant value in going and speaking to people direct. Recently, at The University of Sheffield, UK, this was done through a 'conversational tour' of all departments in the institution.

Framing the conversations

In order to undertake a qualitative adventure of this size (at our institution, 46 departments through 26 two-hour conversations), it is important to devise a conversational tool that will enable efficiency and consistency, be relevant to the sector and resonate with the audience. Use of a sector document – for example the UK's Concordat to Support the Career Development of Researchers ('Concordat') – is advisable to ensure a commonly understood framework that looks at the researcher from a holistic perspective.

Who to converse with

The researcher does not exist in a vacuum, so the voices of research managers and supporters of research (Concordat terms) are also valuable to the process. Senior colleagues drive the culture that researchers exist in, so involving them in the conversation lays the foundation for collective engagement in culture change. In this case, 129 people contributed directly to the institution's tour, including 57 researchers, some of them canvassing other colleagues' opinions prior to the scheduled conversations.

The logistics of going 'on tour'

Well-honed event management skills are needed for an undertaking of this magnitude. If you have only one person available to go on tour, there is a need for complete immersion in this task and to view it as a longitudinal process that will involve preparation, planning and delivery in the short term, much writing up, and – in the longer term – impact review that explores any change, no matter how incremental.

Two considerations

Having the process endorsed at committee level, ideally by a pro vice-chancellor for research (or similarly titled equivalent) and supported by faculty leaders for research gives you a much better chance of engaging other senior colleagues with the process. Endorsement also underpins success when it comes to implementation of any emerging recommendations or suggestions for culture shift.

Tenacity is needed to chase up those unacknowledged emails, reinforce the value of such in-depth consultation, and to make the process happen.

Benefits

1) For the conversing researcher developer, the process in *itself* is an excellent opportunity for relationship building, myth dispelling, breaking down barriers and generally reinforcing the importance of researchers and their development.
2) For the conversers en masse, it is an opportunity not only to discuss researchers but more broadly the research landscape, the challenges in creating a supportive and inclusive environment and the achievements: an opportunity to celebrate good practice and share ideas.

3) The action of having the conversation subtly states the institution's position — if there is dedicated conversation about the need to support and develop researchers, then logically it must be an area of import.

4) The outputs can be used to develop common standards. In our institution, core recommended practices have been agreed at all levels that have collective buy-in.

Bryony Portsmouth

Complementary ideas include **7** and **48**.

3 Doing more with less

The explosion of formalised development for researchers has dramatically raised expectations within the research community of the support that might be offered. Accelerated by governmental drivers and their attached funding, the rise of Doctoral Training Centres and Networks, and higher education institutions (HEIs) trying to compete internationally and boost impact, the demand for researcher development activity, in the UK and internationally, is at an all-time high. However, in an austere financial climate, how can the development community match raised expectation with minimal or minimised funding? In short, how can we do more with less?

Define 'more'

First, what does 'more' mean to you as a researcher developer? Increased headcount? Better programme engagement? Maximised value added? Re-examine your core mission and think 'what is this effort for?' If activity means 'workshops', then 'more' inevitably leads to an increase in headcount per event, and thus perhaps a reduction of quality of developmental experience. Maybe we need to think again.

Re-examine your resources

Much innovative development activity in the UK can be found within institutions which were always research-council-cash poor. So, where is your resource strength? Is it your networks? Your supportive academics? Your community links? Your joined-up pathways from PhD through research staff through academic development programmes? Sometimes, simply sharing information effectively reveals low-hanging fruit. For instance, I am frequently asked to run the same workshop three times by the same organisation for three different levels of researcher – none of whose programme managers have the faintest idea what is going on in other areas of their university.

Look around for resources that are available but that you're not using. Are your academics actively involved in your programmes? Not just at a committee oversight level, but actually contributing to the researcher experience? A half-hour Q&A panel with experienced role models can add huge value – and it costs very little.

Amplify your impact

Often in industry it is expected that every employee discuss their development needs with their manager, thus ensuring alignment of individual and larger need. It's also often required that individuals formally share ('trickle down') their learning with their teams and so increase overall value. Does this happen at your place? The rise of cohort-based training models, research clusters, discipline centres and other collaboration facilitators offers more possibilities for increased trickle-down.

Principal investigators and doctoral supervisors are often unaware of what occurs in the development community and so potential researcher impacts can be lost. However, development that is aligned with the institution's academic development offerings may lead to far greater impact. (For example, many HEIs run a researcher induction and also a supervisor training course. Do we take care to align these offerings?)

Information or development?

How much of your offering is based around 'information'? Policy, rules, regulations and codes of practice can be put online. Much of the 'development' that occurs in our institutions is actually information-based, and this can be ramped up using technology, flipped learning or larger group delivery.

Real 'development' means getting people out of their silos and sharing practice. Helping researchers to grow communities of practice (mentoring; peer support; self-perpetuating action learning sets) where the focus is the process of learning how to do research – not just presentations of research data – offers huge sustainable value.

Develop the developer capacity

How reliant are you on external expertise or academic time? A 'develop the developer' programme for (e.g.) research staff can mean that elements of your PhD programme can be delivered sustainably, and your research staff develop facilitation and presentation skills.

Prove your organisational worth

Finally, ask yourself what value your programme actually adds strategically to your organisation. If we could truly evidence the genuine value to our organisation – not bums-on-seats metrics or immediate-response feedback – then maybe we wouldn't be in the position of having 'less' to do 'more' with.

Steve Hutchinson

Complementary ideas include **7**, **45** and **51**.

4 Should development activities be compulsory?

'You need to do more exercise!'

Even if I were your best friend, such a forthright statement would probably not make you head straight to the gym. Most of us don't like being told what to do!

The same is true when developing researchers. Forcing them to do development activities is generally counterproductive. If they engage, they just go through the motions, treating it as a tick-box exercise.

Workshops may not be the answer
Successful development activities should have long-term impact, and that is very unlikely if the people attending don't want to be there. It's all too easy to think that attending a couple of workshops is sufficient. To have genuine impact, an activity needs to help identify strengths and weaknesses, and enable actions to be planned and followed through. Otherwise the opportunity for growth is missed. We want to see new habits formed that enable the individual to be more effective and successful in fulfilling their long-term goals. In the research context, a supervisor or principal investigator has a vital role to play. In the best case, they encourage and release their researchers to seize the opportunities available; in the worst case, development may be almost impossible.

Everyone is unique
We're all different! We have different skills and abilities, experiences and interests. Each researcher will necessarily have different development needs. Some sort of reflection to consider needs and options, whether through a formal training needs analysis or not, helps to ensure the training someone undertakes will actually be useful.

If we want researchers to develop particular skills or competencies, we need to make it easy for them to engage. In a university, any target audience for development activities will encompass a wide range of personal situations, life experiences, disciplinary expertise and learning styles. By allowing people to select the development activities they need, at the time which fits with their life(style) and ideally by offering a range of ways for them to 'consume' it, you create an environment that is more likely to help researchers change their practice and behaviour.

But more than that, we want people to address their development needs in the way that will be most effective for them. That might even mean they do something outside the university, entirely of their own devising – volunteering for a charity, a few hours' part-time work, giving a talk at a local school. A compulsory training programme discourages people from addressing their needs in a personalised way.

Do compulsory activities ever work?
Sometimes people need to know certain things – legal and ethical standards, for example – but this doesn't apply to most development needs.

There is a growing tension between voluntary and compulsory development activities, exemplified by the doctoral training centres/partnerships proliferating in the UK (where funding for doctoral training is increasingly allocated through block training grants for annual cohorts, typically of 5–50 students). The development programmes that are a standard part of these centres may contain a number of compulsory initiatives. These focus on core skills such as those described in the development frameworks found in many sectors. The argument is that funders and researcher developers know the skills early career researchers need to have. It will be interesting to see the long-term impact of these programmes. I suspect the added benefit of doing activities with the same group of people each time, and the relationships that are developed, may work to overcome any apathy caused by their compulsory nature. We shall see.

My advice would be to pick any development initiatives you choose to make compulsory with great care, and to evaluate the long-term impacts on the researchers.

Nigel Eady

Complementary ideas include **1** and **10**.

5 Professionalising participant behaviour

When I started to lead programmes outside of academia I was amazed when participants were early, had done the preparatory work and had clear development objectives. Oddly, I was *surprised* by professionalism. Yes, HEIs are places where we can convince ourselves that many corporate 'rules' don't apply; but all researchers *are* professionals. High fees, though, lead to high expectations, and our status as 'service' departments means that we encounter behaviours that academic teaching colleagues wouldn't tolerate (*Er, sorry I'm an hour late. Yes, it's a full-day thing, but I want to leave before lunch. Also, I want all the notes...*). This obviously isn't the majority of cases — but it's disruptive and may indicate a patchy disrespect, or an inability to recognise that researcher developers add genuine academic value.

This problem may start with the institution. For instance, is it easy to book rooms for researcher development? If we're last in the queue then it's only natural that we find ourselves justifying our worth. Is every *single* event on your programme measured with 'happy-sheet' (immediate response) feedback to within an inch of its life? Why? Does every iota of these data lead to programme improvement?

Because of our perceived status, I believe the researcher development community has pandered and indulged non-professional behaviour because we are desperate for the academy to *like us*. If this means we chase high immediate scores (as opposed to *valuable* long-term feedback), then we're likely to ignore 'bad' behaviour to ensure maximised happy sheets (*Two hours late? Never mind, come in!*).

At root, 'development' means *support* (which we offer abundantly) and *challenge* (which we typically don't — because it doesn't get good short-term feedback). The most useful piece of 'development' feedback I've ever had was from a tutor who challenged me for dominating a discussion. In time, the feedback was invaluable, but – short-term – I *hated* him. Given an immediate-feedback form I'd have lowered his average forever! Redefine your feedback form mechanisms, so as to avoid chasing numerical scores. If every single offering is continually scrutinised, this must – at some level – signal a lack of institutional trust; and perhaps propagate a consumerist lack of respect from participants?

I think we must acknowledge that developers want to deliver a programme that researchers both need and engage with. This requires that we work alongside our participants and make feedback mechanisms less about ourselves and more about reflections and discussions of what was actually learned and inspired in the longer term.

So, to remedy the behaviour of the minority, we must consider what professionalism means and make this explicit up front. Sometimes our participants have genuine reasons for 'non-professionalism' – but many don't. We need an explicit system that differentiates. (A colleague who locked the door five minutes after a workshop start was accused recently of 'humiliating' a latecomer. If their policy was unclear in advance then I understand the embitterment.) This definition and explanation should be carried out in conjunction with academic role models – after all, monkey see, monkey do. Draw up a list of the behaviours that you'd expect from a professional undertaking development activity (e.g. arrive early; don't constantly check Twitter). Make this 'contract' explicit and reciprocal (*We will... if you will...*).

Consider the effectiveness of your punitive measures. Does fining repeated non-attendance lead to professionalism? Possibly – but more likely it results in non-registration, less throughput and reduced budgets. Billing the supervisor might lead to individual training prohibitions. Charging their department tells the institution that our activity has value.

Participants need to know that our offerings are not an entitlement, but worth effort and investment. 'Development' programmes, however, often commence with an obligatory induction that is frequently information-based, web-accessible and requires no engagement. Is this the right tone for *development*?

Acknowledging perceived obligation (*I know some of you don't want to be here. So, how can we make this useful?*) is a powerful lever and can help a contracting process (*In return, as ground rules I expect…*). Also, frankly, we ourselves need to re-examine our practices. After all, if someone is constantly distracted, then what's occurring in the room isn't too scintillating.

Finally, and vitally, be brave – challenge bad behaviour. If you're a valued professional within your organisation and your expectations are explicit then you should expect that senior management would back your judgement. If they don't, then perhaps we're trying to professionalise the wrong people.

Steve Hutchinson

Complementary ideas include **6** and **15**.

6 Ethics in researcher development

How we engage with researchers needs to be ethically based – treating them fairly and equally, being open, honest and sincere, respecting their confidentiality, but also adhering to institutional or other organisational requirements. This is especially true when we are directly faced with challenging situations.

Example scenarios
Set out below are some examples of tricky situations that might arise, with some initial thoughts as to how they could be addressed. It would be worth discussing these and your own examples with colleagues, to consider in advance how you might handle them.

A supervisor asks about a specific participant who was in a workshop you led
While the tone and context of the conversation will be crucial, the starting point has to be to clarify the confidentiality that was established within the workshop. It should also be remembered that the question might even be 'Was my researcher in the session?'– whether to check they are accessing the support they should, or to find out if they've been wasting time not being in the lab/office, or something in between. On this matter, I would simply refer to whatever the administrative procedures are for recording attendance, since they should be governed by their own confidentiality rules. On anything more substantive, I would speak in general terms about the topics that the workshop covered, and potentially the range of responses from the participant group, but I would not go beyond this. Instead, I would encourage the supervisor to discuss the workshop directly with the researcher.

One participant rubbishes the research of another
If there is personal history involved, then this is an area I would simply try to avoid being drawn into, and encourage the

participants to continue their discussion outside the workshop. Otherwise, this situation could be a source of considerable learning, especially where the views come from differences in discipline, methodology, paradigm, etc. Depending on the topic of the workshop, I may well choose to explore the views expressed in a scenario, such as:

- What exactly are your objections, from a research perspective? How might the research be adjusted to overcome these?
- OK, Freda doesn't see the value of Bob's research: imagine she is on the review panel (or ethics committee or appointment board). How might we make Bob's case so as to persuade her?

A researcher admits to falsifying a result in a proposal, paper or thesis
It will matter whether this is disclosed in plenary, small group or one-to-one. And clearly the scale and extent of falsification will also be crucial. If confidentiality has been established, then clearly there can be no suggestion of reporting back. As such, it will fall to you to pose questions as to the potential consequences. The balance is in whether it falls to you to pass judgment or not? I tend to assume not. Just as I can't know enough to tell a supervisor how to supervise a particular researcher, or a member of research staff how to get a fellowship, so I can't tell a researcher what they have done is wrong. But I would feel able to suggest what I think the consequences of actions might be, and I do feel able to express what I think I would do in a given situation.

How do you engage with development related to a topic or political agenda with which you disagree?
Start with a disclaimer! I try to establish at the outset of any workshop the precise aims of it, and these rarely include 'critiquing the government policy on…' or 'redesigning the way X funder distributes their money'. As such, my approach is always to be explicit: our purpose is to enable the participants to achieve the best that they can in the given environment. We can do that without having to endorse or approve of that environment. Rather than try to ignore a major political issue in the room, a small

Ethics in researcher development **6**

space to 'let off steam', where necessary, can help defuse things. But these spaces need to be carefully limited, and there is always the likelihood that not everyone in attendance will be of the same view.

Final thoughts

I am sure you will have had strong reactions to each scenario, and may well disagree with my approach. Great. The purpose is to start thinking about these things before they arise, so that if they ever do, you are already in a position to respond ethically and wisely to them.

Dave Filipović-Carter

Complementary ideas include **18**.

7 Researcher development in the institutional context: exerting influence

Think about system and structure

We research developers often rail against the institution and the culture within which we are working as if they are the enemy, instead of seeking to understand the complex systems and structures that our key stakeholders are involved in and thereby identify leverage points – those points within a system where you may be able to exert influence to get what you need or want.

We often complain, for example, that supervisors are not engaged with the wider development of their researchers beyond the things that will lead to getting more papers published, doctoral theses completed and contribute to success as defined for research in the academic culture. So it is important that we consider how to demonstrate the contribution we make to the goals that the system rewards. Can we provide evidence, for example, that students complete their theses on time if they engage in wider development beyond research-specific skills? How does the impact of our work demonstrably add value regarding the pressures academic supervisors and departments face? Can we demonstrate how our work aligns and adds value to the strategic priorities and performance indicators set by the university?

Engage structurally

It is important for researcher developers to understand the structures of the organisation that they work in and to communicate that understanding to researchers – particularly those interested in pursuing academic careers. Most universities involve complex hierarchies and committee structures which can seem baffling and as though they were established with the specific aim of tripping you up and preventing you from achieving things for your researchers. Don't make the mistake of being discouraged by this – the committee structures and hierarchies need to be your friends and not your enemies. Committees in particular can be formed of very powerful people in universities and getting a seat at this table – or at least a regular paper on the agenda – can be highly beneficial. Influencing committees can help you get more things done, obtain important support for new initiatives and boost the profile of researcher development within the organisation.

Role model what you teach

In order for researchers to progress in their academic careers, they need to learn early on how to engage with structures, find the leverage points in systems, deal with institutional politics and show leadership. You can help them by finding out as much as you can about how your university works and where it fits into the wider systems and structures in the environment of which it is a part. Demonstrating how you can use this knowledge to get things done is an important exemplar for your researchers – they can learn by seeing what you do as well as from the information you pass onto them.

Questions for you to think about

To help you exert influence in your organisation, consider the following questions:

- How can you map your work into your organisation's drivers and key objectives?
- How can you choose the right language to communicate that what you do is aligned to the business of academia and your university?
- What else do you need to do in order to understand the systems and structures of the organisation you work for and to identify the leverage points you can use? Do you need help from other people in your university who seem to understand these things better? Would they make a good mentor for you?

Fiona Denney

Complementary ideas include **2** and **9**.

8 Accrediting your researcher development programme

Why accredited provision?

One of the first questions anyone considering accrediting programmes should ask is: why bother? The accreditation process is demanding in a number of ways. In brief, the answer to 'why' can be summed up in the benefits it offers for its two main stakeholders: the institution and researchers themselves.

For the institution, researcher development provides meaningful support for researchers and increases research capacity. Achieving accreditation ensures a high level of quality assurance and provides legitimacy. For researchers, this legitimacy is key and one of the main drivers for engagement with researcher development. Accredited programmes also reward engagement with recognition: a certificate, diploma, or master's degree. Researchers' efforts are, thus, validated and documented. This recognition is useful for progression internally and when applying for positions externally.

What's involved?

It requires considerable time and investment to develop an accredited programme. The programme at the University of Strathclyde, for example, took roughly 24 months to realise in full. When designing an accredited programme, a crucial first step is to engage stakeholders so as to determine interest and need, and to identify support and opportunities for collaboration. Information gathered from stakeholders should inform the business case for accreditation. A business case is usually required by internal and external funding bodies.

Considering the larger-scale structures that will make up your curricula, an important debate to have is whether to use closed or open pathways. Closed pathways limit participants to a set menu of modules. Alternatively, open pathways allow for a measure of choice, providing an à la carte menu of modules for the participants to choose from. Both options have their benefits: closed pathways are simple, easy to manage and maintain – and might therefore be easier to accredit – whereas open pathways are more complex, but can be more dynamic and provide participants with greater means to steer their own development.

In terms of costing the programme, the largest expense comes from personnel. Even with the smallest of programmes, consideration should be given to sustainable workload requirements: development, delivery, evaluation and administration time must be duly counted. Additionally, initial or ongoing fees might be required by the external accreditor.

Achieving accreditation
For most institutions, internal accreditation is achieved through a central or faculty body. For example, at Strathclyde, internal accreditation is handled through the School of Education. Keep in mind when planning programmes that accrediting bodies – both internal and external – have rigid structures that must be followed, particularly regarding module and programme approval. It is also worth being aware of the timing(s) of accreditation events in the academic calendar.

The actual act of accrediting programmes internally is normally a matter of presenting a business case for the programme to the relevant body and then working with them to realise the programme. Relationship-building is extremely important. Be responsive and adaptive.

Finding an external accreditor is by far the greater challenge. There remain few bodies in the UK or beyond capable of accrediting researcher development programmes – although this might be changing. Ideally the relationship between the programme and its external accreditor should derive from mutual benefit. Such is the case currently with the Strathclyde MSc where accreditation of researcher development modules allows more researchers to acquire Fellowship of the Higher Education Academy (HEA).

Conclusion

A large number of factors need to be considered in developing and running an accredited programme. A successful accredited programme brings with it a great deal of opportunities for the institution, for researchers and for developers, but it also presents challenges that need to be carefully managed to ensure benefit for all and the continued sustainability of the programme.

Stuart Boon and Fiona Conway

Complementary ideas include **15** and **18**.

Chapter 2
Fundamentals of researcher development

9 Golden rules of researcher development

Golden rule 1
Enjoy what you do. The best researcher development is life changing, and that is a wonderful privilege to be a part of. Other rules:

Think holistically
Researcher development is more than a training workshop; it encompasses any opportunity to support personal or professional development. Think about the environment (internal and external) within which your activity is situated and how it can work best within that environment. It may be that working to influence something within the environment in which your professional development is situated has a larger effect on the success of your activity than altering a training workshop in isolation. So think about...

Stakeholder engagement
Know your stakeholders, what they think, want and need. Ask, don't assume. Do you know the people you stand in front of? Are you embedded in your institution's committee structures, processes, systems, etc.?

Staff and skills
Do you have the skills? Are you a personal and professional development advocate by example?

Research or evidence-based practice
From what basis of knowledge are you providing activity? Can you evidence the impact of your practice? Universities are about the creation, dissemination and application of knowledge. Do all three!

Profile and awareness

Do all stakeholders (internal and external) know you, what you do and why your agenda matters? Network; for example, attend UK conferences such as the Vitae Researcher Development International Conference and the Researcher Education and Development Scholarship Conference, or, in Australia, the Quality in Postgraduate Research Conference. Get involved in your national or international organisation.

Strategy

What is the plan (for the benefit of each stakeholder)? How does developing one group of people help to meet wider strategic needs (i.e. of the organisation)? How are you going to deliver the plan?

Know your policy area and your researchers

Understand how the sector is moving. Be aware of the thinking of research funders and employers. But most importantly of all, understand the researchers you are developing. Be proactive. How can the profession improve? What will you do to shape these agendas?

Now… training and development programmes:

The programme

Create programmes that reflect all of the above. Design with purpose to achieve outcomes that stakeholders care about. For any development challenge ask, *What is the best way to achieve skills development for the researcher?* If the 'answer' is 'a workshop', great, go for it! If it is not, don't be afraid to do something different.

Make sure tailoring for an individual need is possible. There will be most interest in provision that is considered core to an immediate need. Something perceived to be non-core will need more reasoning and evidencing. Alternatively, if you can't demonstrate that it is core to stakeholder need, why are you doing it? Don't simply copy provision from elsewhere. Think about how it will work in your environment.

Facilitating

Yes, prepare well, plan thoroughly, but observe the group. No two groups are the same mix of personalities, learning preferences, etc. Be ready to be flexible because observation may tell you, *Today we need to do this differently!* Take a risk or two, and if it goes wrong, learn from it rather than worry about it.

Final golden rule

Be proud of what you do, because you matter; and more than sometimes, you might be appreciated.

Tony Bromley

Complementary ideas include **2**, **7** and **15**.

10 Setting out on the right foot: development from induction onwards

For many researcher developers the first contact with our target audience, whether staff or student, is at formal induction. In our experience, this was usually a peripheral slot, low down on the running order, with an already-overloaded audience.

However, as developers we should endeavour to be *central* to induction, thus ensuring a developmental theme. Such a placement offers an enormous return for the effort involved.

Induction – the rationale

Is induction to welcome individuals to the academic community? Or to ensure that certain compliance boxes have been ticked? Most right-minded professionals would suggest the former is appropriate, but many inductions end up as the latter. And regardless of the induction category (institutional, faculty, department), it is important to remember just how isolating research can be. As such, induction must balance the introduction of key information with actually allowing networks to propagate.

An academic induction that one of the authors attended had presentations from two senior professors. The first opined 'you should *want* to win a Nobel Prize'; the second that 'you probably *won't* get an academic job'. This caused discussion and debate, bringing important issues into the open. As developers, we should both help clarify researcher expectations and also help broach the subject of a road map for the future – starting with an individual's success in mind. An exploration of how their new undertaking differs from any previous one may offer a useful bridge to the notion that what has brought success so far won't necessarily work in future. Useful allies are *well chosen* voices of experience. Junior academics who have had positive experiences of researcher development and who will say the 'right' things with hindsight, can offer huge value.

Induction – the process
Here we must separate the induction *process* (everything from payroll information to ethical conformity) from an induction *event*. Any institutional induction will need to deal with both the big pictures (university culture, values, strategy) and little ones (library facilities and IT support). Yet we must ask ourselves: *How do you want them to feel at the end of the process?*

Do you want participants to have passively received information or do you want to have individuals engaged and already actively involved in planning their own development?

With this in mind, how should an induction event work? Should it be staged in large groups (efficient and good networking possibilities, but generic content), small groups (tailored, but time-consuming and potentially isolationist) or even individual (personalised but with huge workload implications and straying into supervisorial responsibilities)?

Should it be compulsory or optional? The institutionally 'obvious' answer is that induction must be compulsory – but this response is probably concerned with compliance and information provision. Compulsory information can be put online (and monitored). A 'special' event to which people are *invited* will foster a more developmental spirit. As with most developmental activity, success is linked to the buy-in or engagement of supervisors and principal investigators, and compulsion is rarely an academically winning tactic.

Given that induction happens over a period of time, it is worth thinking of it as a series of stages. What do researchers need before they start? (You may find a huge difference in the pre-start needs of international researchers versus those who are based in your country already.) What do they need during the first month? Is there scope and space for a follow-on session in six months' time?

Setting out on the right foot **10**

We should also consider what happens *after* our researchers leave the event. Even if event legacy is a signposting resource with a 'now do this' checklist, our efforts will not be wasted once 'actual research' starts.

Induction – the content

When selecting appropriate content, it's imperative to consider the needs of the new starters, and even to canvass what inductees are confused about *before* the event. Involving research supervisors and principal investigators in this reconnaissance may also help achieve buy-in.

Starting a new job or large project is demonstrably stressful, and at such times adults operate and learn on a 'need-to-know' basis. Information overload is thus likely to be counterproductive. Ask, *What content is needed right now, what can be saved for later?*

Research induction is likely to involve specialist partners (human resources, research office, library, etc.), but do inductees need lengthy presentations, or merely to meet faces? A brief introduction (and a presentation limited to three top tips) from specialist partners combined with stalls that inductees can canvass over lunch, is much more likely to build a healthy relationship for when someone actually has a need-to-know moment later on.

Finally, we believe that the essential elements of a successful induction (staff or student) are that people:

- feel involved, integrated and welcomed members of the academic community;
- sense that they are valued as part of the wider institutional mission;
- understand multi-lateral responsibilities and consider good professional habits;
- receive opportunities to commence strong and productive networks;

- realise that self-development is key to research success and have ideas on how to achieve ownership of this activity.

And then...? Well, that's when the real work starts.

Steve Hutchinson, Kay Guccione and Rob Daley

Complementary ideas include **1**, **4** and **45**.

11 Supporting researchers to take control of their personal development

Researcher development programmes within universities are often workshop based, providing a range of short events in support of transferable skills development. While there is definitely a place for workshops with an emphasis on the acquisition of knowledge and skills, personal development is so much more than this.

As researcher developers we should be supporting researchers to take control of their personal development more broadly. This life skill supports not only the development of skills, but also the development of self-awareness, talents and potential.

What does it mean for researchers to take control of their personal development?
Taking control means asking the following questions:

* What are my career and development goals?
* What do I *want* and *need* to develop in terms of knowledge, skills and behaviours?
* How do I prefer to learn and what might I gain from challenging these preferences from time to time?
* How do I find and structure the most appropriate development opportunities for me?
* What support do I need to manage my personal development? Who could act as an effective mentor or coach for me in this regard?
* From where do I get my feedback? How do I know my strengths and weaknesses as others see them?

As researcher developers we should be the *facilitators* of learning. In practice, this means we *educate* researchers on learning and the management of their personal development, we *support* them to create structured learning opportunities, we *advise* them on how to give and receive developmental feedback, and we *encourage* them to reflect on themselves.

In gastronomic terms, rather than operate as waiters 'serving up' a banquet of events, we should be the chefs de cuisine supporting researchers to create a personalised 'menu' of learning that suits their goals and preferences. In so doing, we empower them to take control of their personal development, both now and in the future.

How should we design researcher development programmes to support this approach?

In addition to the provision of skills workshops, we could add the following interventions to our programmes:

Educational materials and briefing sessions on personal development and learning
These sessions should challenge traditional assumptions and approaches within higher education as it relates to personal learning. Experiential learning should be explained and contrasted with traditional teaching methods.

One-to-one personal development support and coaching
We could use focused sessions to supportively challenge researchers through the questions in the previous box and to support them in the creation of structured learning interventions. We could advise them on how to create *integrated* learning opportunities that take place within their academic environments. For example, rather than attend a course on assertiveness, they could create, with our support, opportunities to practise their assertiveness at work. A researcher might choose to become an active member of a committee and could approach a couple of members on the committee for feedback on their communication style.

Extended personal development programmes
Such programmes offer opportunities for students to reflect and to give and receive behavioural feedback.

We could extend a traditional skills workshop to include opportunities for researchers to practise the skill and to then reflect on their approach and receive feedback from others. Two-part split-sessions with two shorter workshops surrounding a period of practice and reflection over a week or two could offer heavily amplified benefits.

In short, workshops have a place in development, and it's likely they always will – but as chefs de cuisine we must be creative about how we use our tried and trusted ingredients.

Heather McGregor

Complementary ideas include **1**, **9**, **12** and **14**.

12 Enhancing self-regulated learning using the 'feedback+' model

Self-regulated learning can be thought of as a person's capacity to actively adapt their thinking and behaviour in order to achieve their desired goals. Research shows that for all types of learners the best performers are the best self-regulated learners. Self-regulation forms the core of how our researchers gain the skills they need to succeed with the PhD and beyond.

There are six key processes that researcher developers can leverage in self-regulated learning: strategy selection; confidence; attention focusing; monitoring; evaluation; and adaptive changes. The good news is that they can all be learned, but crucially, many researchers struggle to develop these processes independently, and require targeted support.

New research in education has found that combining the power of feedback with the concepts of self-awareness and regulation can aid principal investigators and researcher developers to facilitate the development of self-regulated learning. It may only require small modifications to your usual feedback style to make a really big difference. Here is how you can put these principles into practice with researchers as part of workshops or one-to-one sessions.

Enhance your feedback methods
This feedback method is designed to build upon existing good-practice principles and provide something extra; think of it as 'feedback+'. In any feedback situation the researcher needs to leave knowing three basic things:

- Whether or not they have succeeded or failed in the task at hand;
- What specifically they did right and wrong and the reasons why;
- How they can improve for the next attempt (feedforward).

In order to add the '+' we need to find out more about our learner's proficiency in self-regulatory processes. Using this questioning technique will help you target each process in turn, making it an effective way to get fast and accurate information about your learner that you can use to give more specialised feedback.

How do I use it?

Here is an example using a researcher who is practising their presentation.

- Before they begin: ask them questions about their strategy and confidence processes. *How do you plan to make this presentation effective? How confident are you that you will get this right on this practice attempt?*
- During the presentation: stop the learner, focus their attention on the here and now, and check their monitoring. *Are you happy with how this has gone so far? What are you focusing on right now?*
- When they have finished: ask them to evaluate their performance and forward plan. *Why do you think you did/did not deliver it the way you planned? What specific parts about that would you change for next time?*

You can begin to see how you can elicit valuable information on how your learner uses self-regulated learning by simply asking them, using this structured real-time method. This approach is best used as a before-during-after process but can easily be adapted to use retrospectively, or in one-to-one meetings.

The key part is then using the information to mould your feedback message around improving those six main self-regulated learning abilities. This has the aim of helping learners realise and calibrate their self-awareness, in relation to the task.

This method allows the learner to contribute to their own development by 'talking out' their strengths and weaknesses, effectively helping them become more adaptive and reflective.

Billy Bryan

Complementary ideas include 11.

13 What do you call a programme to make it appealing?

Many institutions organise their researcher development provision within an umbrella programme or programmes. Much thought and effort goes into the development of both individual researcher development activities and the design of coherent offerings of workshops and activities to ensure that our researchers have excellent support available to them. Once all the hard work is done there remains one final decision: what should the programme be called? And then the difficulties really begin! This final decision can often prove to be the most difficult and the most divisive of all those involved in researcher development. Below are a few considerations which should guide you to a suitable choice.

The purpose and scope of the programme

Firstly, clearly identify the purpose of the programme, the limits of its content, its central aims – and know what it is not (i.e. what falls outside the programme and will be grouped or advertised elsewhere or in some other manner). Only when you have a clear and shared concept of what your programme is and what it is for will you be able to agree a suitable name.

The audience

Consider the audience carefully – who the core audience is and who else might be interested and included in the programme's wider audience. Try to ensure that the name clearly states to the core audience that this is for them. At the same time, consider whether the name signals that the programme is not suitable for or aimed at other groups who might see the marketing materials and adverts. Anything with 'research' or 'researcher' in the title will automatically resonate with researchers, and will also signal to other stakeholders that these activities are supporting the institutional research effort. Anything with your institution in the name will define it as aimed at your institutional members – great for attracting institutional participants but difficult if you then wish to run a programme collaboratively with another institution.

Sub-programmes
Does the overall programme have groups of activities that naturally fit together? Could or should these have their own collective identity within the wider programme (e.g. induction workshops for doctoral researchers, funding workshops for staff, etc.)? These sub-sets can then have their own mini-marketing campaign and may appeal to participants who are not attracted by the overall programme.

Clashes with other organisations and agendas
Take care to check that your chosen title has not already been taken by any organisation or activity that might bring about confusion. National funders, other research organisations, and even parts of your own organisation may already have, or be planning, activities that would fit well under your chosen name. If these are speaking to similar audiences then it can be detrimental to your message and engagement.

Catchy
A good name is easy to remember and easy to pronounce. However, do check that it doesn't sound or look like any term or phrase in another language. This might be both embarrassing and detrimental. That said, you cannot be expected to check all languages. Think about your institution and the make-up of its members. Some examples of existing programme names include:

- Skills for the Professional Researcher;
- Enhancing Research Practice;
- Research Leaders;
- Preparing Future Academics;
- Postdoc to PI.

13 *What do you call a programme to make it appealing?*

Individual elements

Most of this advice is also valid when naming individual activities and workshops within wider programmes. Some programmes also contain related activities which might benefit from having a group heading (such as 'Successful Supervision' for a set of workshops dealing with the different challenges that supervisors face).

Longevity

Finally, you want a name to stand the test of time. While you cannot future-proof against all eventualities, do take some care to ensure that your institution is not planning a restructuring or merger or anything else that might result in your name needing to be changed. Having gone to all this hard work, you will not want to start all over again.

Rob Daley

Complementary ideas include **46**.

14 Impact beyond the face-to-face session

The aim of a face-to-face (F2F) development session is to impact how researchers work – how they do their research and their other professional activities. But we have so little time to directly influence them. And when we do interact with them, they are away from their normal work setting. We need to make sure that what we do in the limited F2F time will impact on what they do when they are back at work.

Pre-session engagement
Engagement ahead of sessions typically involves a questionnaire to ascertain the researcher's level, need, etc. and limited preparatory work. This can save time on the course and provide a more focused session. But it can go further:

Introductory material
We spend a lot of F2F time dealing with matters that can be pre-delivered – from the mundane introductory material to the deeper engagement aspects. Where there is access to a shared VLE (virtual learning environment), asynchronous forum tasks can easily enable participant introductions, sharing of problems, discussion of common issues, and even early-stage problem-solving. This can then free up on-course time for deeper engagement with core content. Alternatively, email can be used to achieve much of this, or synchronous conferencing software can be used (although that might be a whole new topic).

Troubleshooting
The challenge is that some people won't participate, or that they fail to complete the pre-session work. To an extent, that is their choice – so long as we don't allow that choice to consume F2F time. For example, give a simple acknowledgment of the non-

completion, and the fact that this might disadvantage them during the session, rather than offer to spend time on it during the session. This also emphasises the personal responsibility expected of participants. But there are ways to reduce the likelihood of non-completion:

- Make communication about what is required clear and brief.
- Make the pre-session tasks clear and brief.
- If possible, integrate the tasks with course registration, so that registration is not confirmed until the tasks are completed.
- And, longer term, develop an institutional culture of such requirements, including emphasising the efficiency of this for F2F time.

Real scenarios
Any scenario or case study used on course could be a missed opportunity. By engaging participants ahead of time, it is possible to use genuine examples from them. 'Role play' becomes 'real play', so that discussions and outcomes are useable by participants directly, and are perceived to be more relevant because the situation is a genuine one from someone in the workshop.

In-session relevance
While pre-session engagement can make the workshop activities more relevant to participants, applicability can also be enhanced during the session through careful choice of focus:

Direct relevance to them
When a workshop activity or discussion is explicitly linked to participants' real work it will have greater impact. This relevance can be shown and enhanced by taking participants through an evocation process – drawing out their own ideas before direct input from you. This can also help you to avoid false assumptions, and ensure you use their vocabulary. This will remove some of the need for them to translate your 'general' to their 'specific'. At its simplest, just ask open questions:

- What are the best and worst things about your role(s)?
- Why do you do what you do?
- Why have you come to this session?

Going further, such techniques can generate the scenarios to be solved, frame the questions to be discussed, produce case-study material to be used, and so on.

Begin implementation now

When someone leaves a workshop, the impact of it has to compete with everything else that is going on. And impact fades over time. By bringing the work context into the course, some of this can be reduced.

The later stages of any session should ideally include participants actually undertaking a real implementation task. This will depend on the session content, but examples are: writing the first section of a proposal; drafting a personal statement; or peer reviewing their current online profile. A slightly riskier strategy could involve designing a break from the session to allow participants to return to the lab or office for a fixed time to undertake a defined task, before returning to debrief. The risk is that those outside distractions begin to creep in. But the advantage is that this is even more real. By emphasising the potential benefits of the process, and their responsibility for their own learning, these risks should be minimal. Longer versions could even include email or VLE forum interactions during the practice, to build greater post-session robustness.

Post-session learning

Session impact will always tail off over time, so aim to build momentum straight away.

Keeping going

Any on-course implementation can be continued immediately post-course. Ideally with tight deadlines (tomorrow, this week) to avoid the initial fade. And, if possible, to include the same process that was used in the workshop. For example, this could be a meeting (virtual or F2F) to peer review the piece that has been written; or a 'group review' of the task undertaken, even if it was done alone. Such interaction could even be developed into action learning sets, to move from F2F workshop to autonomous in-work development.

Way points
Momentum can be maintained by self-reminders and prompts. These can be as simple as asking participants to write themselves a postcard during the workshop for later mailing. And many electronic equivalents can be used to increase the sophistication. More dynamic versions can include you or even a colleague or actual principal investigator making a personal intervention.

So what could this look like in practice?
Perhaps the ultimate end point of these developments is that any F2F workshop is situated within a cumulative development process. There may be electronic or F2F interactions either side of the workshop, all supporting autonomous learning processes, including external prompts, guides and reminders. And there is no reason why a range of different researcher developers (academics, central university staff or external consultants) couldn't fit their delivery into such a model.

Dave Filipović-Carter

Complementary ideas include **11** and **18**.

15 How to embed evaluation in your practice

This idea presents a process for the development of any activity with evaluation embedded from the outset. The process is presented in a simplified, practical format, as four question steps, but has a theoretical basis in the 'realist evaluation' approach for those wanting to read further. The steps are best followed as an aspect of the development of a new activity. However, the process can be 'retrofitted' to challenge an existing activity using the following questions, but framed in the past tense.

Question steps

1. *What is the identified professional development issue that your 'activity' will be designed to address?*
If you don't know what the issue is, don't go any further! There is little point evaluating something if there is little idea as to why the activity is taking place. You may need to do pre-work to better understand the issue.

2. *Where are you now in terms of the identified need/issue?*
You need to establish a 'baseline' reference point for the evaluation.

3. *Where would you like to be in terms of the identified need/issue?*
Know what impact or outcomes you are hoping to achieve.

4. *How are you going to get to where you would like to be?*
In practice things change slightly as you develop and implement an activity or activities. However, if you cannot from the outset see any logical steps to take from where you are now to the outcomes you want, you are unlikely to

---

achieve the intended outcomes! Establishing this framework of logical steps also provides you with an understanding of appropriate data collection points. If the implementation and evaluation of an activity is designed well, the required data collection points will become readily apparent.

When you can answer these four questions start implementing the activity.

Further guidelines for an evaluation

1) *Evaluate or validate?* Evaluation is about studying something to gain understanding with a view to continued learning and enhancement. Validation can be simply confirming something. The end-of-workshop participant feedback questionnaire tends to be more about validation than evaluation. *Did the participants find the workshop useful?* 'Yes'. Then the validation has been done, but in evaluation terms nothing has been learned about 'how?' or 'why?' Or, for a learning and teaching workshop required before teaching undergraduates, *Did the required people attend?* 'Yes'. Validated again, but we don't know if they learned anything.

2) *Prioritise.* To evaluate well will take time and effort. Evaluate priorities.

3) Respect the issue of *attribution*. Although direct causality is unlikely to be ultimately proven, consider what evidence can be collected to draw conclusions 'beyond reasonable doubt'.

4) Use multiple *sources.* Don't make a judgement based on only one source of evidence (particularly quantitative evidence).

5) Appreciate the subjective nature of participants' views and have additional *supporting evidence.* If a postgraduate researcher reports that they have improved their project management, a supportive view from their supervisor would give increased confidence in the postgraduate researcher's self-assessed viewpoint. We are not always good at self-assessing!

6) Do not ignore *unintended/unexpected outcomes* that become apparent during an evaluation. They may be valuable and help focus future or new activity.

How to embed evaluation in your practice **15**

7) Track something through the framework of logical steps: e.g. follow a group of people through the activity and note their perspectives along the way.

8) Have robust *data collection*. Standard methods such as interview, focus group or survey may be all that are needed, but they need to be done correctly for your analysis to be valid. Aim for publishable standards in your practice.

Tony Bromley

Complementary ideas include **26** and **42**.

Chapter 3
From novice to
professional researcher

16 Defining 'doctorateness': setting the goal for the PhD

The meaning of 'doctorateness' is a recurring debate that needs to be re-visited regularly. Visions of what 'doctorateness' is may vary from student to supervisor to department. It is important that these should not remain tacit and implicit but should be discussed and debated across development activities, in order that the end goal of the degree is transparent and understood. Even if we cannot fully define the term, we should look for similarities across the diversity of doctorates now established, to search for a better understanding.

Below are four lenses that can be used to focus in on various candidate qualities, motivations, processes and expectations. These can help us to consider how we attract, engage, position and develop research students.

Lens 1: the purpose of pursuing a doctorate?
For some students, reasons may be intrinsic: motivated by a drive for personal development and achievement, or a need to 'prove oneself'. Similarly, motivation might be viewed in terms of satisfying a personal and lasting curiosity or intellectual interest, or drive to find answers.

Extrinsic motivations include career advancement or access, or a way to develop professional practice by researching one's own specialist area. Some students regard a doctorate as a vehicle for development of a set of higher transferable skills relevant to future employment, and contribution to the knowledge economy.

Lens 2: process or product?
The value of the doctorate might be seen in terms of its product – for example, pushing forward the boundaries of knowledge by

generating research outputs, or as manufacturing a high-quality graduate with benchmarked skills, who can be transferred to industry or other sectors.

Or is it about the *process* of personal growth and development, preparation for professional careers, embedding researcher 'ways of being', and apprenticeship to a trade?

Lens 3: doctorateness in written regulations?

We can explore perceptions and articulations of 'doctorateness' by analysing written regulations. All universities have guideline/charter/code of practice documents for students, supervisors and examiners.

Diverse lists of criteria, skills, attributes and behaviours related to doctorateness are available and perform different functions. Some refer to the product, e.g. 'high-class graduates', 'highly employable', or 'world-leading researchers'. Some refer to processes, e.g. 'systematic study', 'rounded development', or 'research training programmes'. Some refer to the qualities, abilities or even dispositions of the student, e.g. 'the best or brightest', 'critical ability', 'competence' or 'high achieving'.

Lens 4: the quest for originality

The two most common thesis-assessment criteria that surface for doctoral degrees are: is it 'worthy of publication'? and is it 'an original work or addition to knowledge'? The concept that poses most anxiety is originality, which we can define for students in at least five ways:

- Sharing new knowledge;
- Using original approaches;
- Creating new syntheses;
- Exploring new implications for practice, policy or theory;
- Contributing new evidence towards recurrent issues or debates.

Where does this leave us?
From my experience of examining doctorates, the single most necessary quality that makes a piece of work a doctorate is the

notion of a 'contribution', without the complication of the adjective 'original' or even 'publishable'.

We need to advise students to consider: Does your doctoral thesis have a position and an argument? Has it built on previous literature and pushed it forward a little? Does it provide another 'brick in the wall'? Will it bring about a change in thinking and to theory, policy or practice?

My view is that a search for an 'inner' meaning is wasted. However, we do owe it to students, supervisors, examiners and employers to help remove the mystique and to make explicit the descriptions and characteristics of doctorateness throughout all development frameworks and programmes.

Jerry Wellington

Complementary ideas include **44**.

17 Supporting researcher identity formation

Why do we need to support identity formation?
As postgraduate research students negotiate transformative learning activities they often don't realise that they will require an identity makeover, which will inevitably change their status in social and academic communities. This constantly brings opportunities for identity formation and for challenges to established identities. You can strategically tailor support activities for nurturing expert researcher identities, and reduce the impending threat posed by 'imposter' feelings.

How is this achieved?
You need to consider 'imposter syndrome': what it is, and how lessons learned from theories of identity formation can be translated into our strategic thinking when designing research support activities.

Imposter syndrome is the main threat to expert identity formation and it is natural for it to be experienced when confidence levels dip. It's a feeling that you 'don't belong'; 'some clerical error or other mistake has been made'; and 'one day you'll be found out with inevitable humiliation'. Students and even established researchers admit to feeling this way from time to time, so it appears to be a natural part of critical reflective practice and scenario planning. So, how do you counterbalance this to help students negotiate transformative learning experiences?

Theories on learner identity reveal that identities are formed in and between actions. Expert or professional identities are fostered by being part of a team, interacting with the environment, and recognition of success. So, how can we translate this into our strategic thinking?

We can encourage researchers to 'feel like an expert researcher', 'be the expert researcher', and 'have recognition of being an expert researcher'.

Feel like an expert researcher
Researcher identities can be formed through a sense of belonging to the research community. By associating with others in the research community and the functions that the community undertake, researchers believe that their own aspirations are being fulfilled:

- *Suggested strategy*: to nurture sustainable peer support networks;
- *Result*: students have expressed feelings of immediate success and recognise that their status has changed in central induction programmes because of their new network.

Be the expert researcher
Researcher identities are developed by practice (in events). By generating a bank of research-based success narratives, positive multiple 'short-term' identities can be established. The level of these successes is modulated by the relationships between the researcher, the research culture and the environment:

- *Suggested strategy*: to develop a more vibrant research culture;
- *Result*: students claim coaching, mentoring and peer discussions support this.

Have recognition of being an expert researcher
Researcher identities are embedded by recognition (across events). The co-recognition of success by others and oneself is important for the incorporation of short-term identities into a long-term 'generalised' schema resulting in a transformational change in status to the expert or professional researcher:

- *Suggested strategy*: to raise the profile of your students as valued members of the researcher community;
- *Result*: students claim that their profile is important for establishing their credibility outside of the university.

And confidence is everything

Cultivate confidence for students to work through vulnerable times as they become experts.

Mark Proctor

Complementary ideas include **19**, **20** and **24**.

18 Using a research-based learning module to enhance doctoral development

Responding to development challenges
We have faced two common challenges in designing programmes of researcher development activities. The first is balancing the need for transferability to varied workplaces with the need for researchers to find programmes relevant and valuable in their immediate work. The second is in how to engage those who are not on campus full time. This idea outlines how we tackled these challenges at the University of the West of England.

Bridging the divide between subject relevance and development activities
In 2012, we launched an optional 'research-based learning' module – Research in Contemporary Context. Inspired by the ideas of work-based learning used to develop professional practices, we developed an analogous concept for doctoral candidates who in the course of their 'work' (research project) must also develop a 'professional practice' (research competencies and behaviours). After interacting in the module with both dedicated and elective workshops drawing on a researcher development framework, participants create a reflective portfolio and case study for assessment. Participants critically reflect on how taught topics impact on their own project, research environment or discipline, emphasising their relevance.

Engaging off-campus learners
The key to making the module accessible is how it is delivered. We use flexible online resources, video conferencing, discussion spaces and session recording to allow remote-location researchers to participate in the workshops, either in real time, or by playback. All module materials are hosted on a virtual learning environment, and assessment and feedback processes are also delivered in this way.

So what? How does this actually enhance researcher development?
Firstly, it embeds each researcher's professional development within their research context, interweaves the two, and challenges the idea that 'time out is time wasted'. In this way it actively engages doctoral supervisors in student development. This is because students have to discuss the module with their supervisor in relation to their research context and development needs. Supervisors also help to assess the portfolios.

Secondly, students get 30 master's-level credits for the module. We think this not only helps with engagement but also provides a recognised and transferable, professional development outcome.

Thirdly, by providing fully interactive, flexible and inclusive access to the learning and reflective activities the module provides.

Lessons and recommendations
The value of this module is very evident in many of the portfolios submitted over the past four years, which demonstrate a high level of engagement with current and critical issues in research that are raised by the module. In particular, reflections on doctoral success criteria, on research integrity matters, and on what it means to be engaged in research work.

The module is part of formal institutional feedback and review processes, enabling us to learn about how it is perceived and engaged with. This has helped to highlight that researchers particularly value the accessibility and flexibility of the module, and the opportunity it affords to discuss important topics in cross-disciplinary groups. Overall, after four cohorts of 15–20 doctoral candidates we think that the module's focus on linking development activities to researchers' projects, involving supervisors, and making use of institutional infrastructures has benefited our doctoral students and enhanced our approach to delivered development activities.

Paul Spencer and Neil Willey

Complementary ideas include **14**, **19** and **45**.

18 Using a research-based learning module   60

19 Developing critical repertoires in doctoral students

The traditional relationship between a doctoral student and supervisor is one of power differential, often characterised as a master–apprentice, expert–novice relationship. This thinking traps supervisory relationships in a 'transmission' or 'training' style, with students on the receiving end of instruction from experts. Indeed, the notion of 'supervisor', as opposed to alternatives like 'advisor', implies asymmetry in the relationship and constructs positions and identities for both parties. Disciplines where supervisors decide the area of research, rather than this coming from the students' own interests, can be particularly problematic.

A decentred approach

In the doctoral programme I direct, we have worked hard to rethink our practice and build a collaborative, collegial approach to developing students. This begins by cultivating a 'decentred' approach to supervision relationships. I argue that doctoral development is an enculturation process, through which students learn about the community they are joining, its history, its key debates, as well as its culture and discourses. Supervisors can be helped to develop this approach through supervisor development activities and departmental initiatives.

In working with doctoral students, supervisors can learn how to construct ways of valuing their students' expertise and academic contributions, and to facilitate the process of induction into the academic community, through a notion of 'critical inclusion'. Critical inclusion is based on collaborative relationships, and we support supervisors to think carefully about the practical and emotional impact of their supervisory styles. We advocate moving beyond a transactional 'tips and techniques' approach to one whereby students are invited into the discourse.

Building research repertoires

On this foundation, we build development of research literacies. Our job is not to 'skill-up' learners but to help them develop the repertoire of a successful member of the academic community – one that mirrors established professional norms, ways of being, and ways of doing research work.

Each person's repertoire will differ in different contexts/disciplines and is more than just a measurable list of competencies. Doctoral students, in current super-diverse times, engage with a broad variety of networks, communities and resources and learn through many different trajectories, tactics and technologies to form a distributed patchwork of competencies, skills, dispositions and values. A student's doctoral repertoire will be biographical, reflecting who they are, where they come from, and what they bring to their research.

Implications for researcher development professionals

To cultivate a decentred approach to doctoral development at institutional level, some useful activities researcher developers could include are: facilitating supervisors' acknowledgment/ valuing of students' expertise; encouraging supervisors to shift the process/language of 'training needs analysis' to one which raises awareness of 'doctoral repertoire'; thinking beyond 'skills' to students' dispositions and values; and fostering reflection on the research culture.

Helping supervisors acknowledge the development of repertoire involves constant negotiation and reflection on students' portfolios; researcher developers can help supervisors recognise the value of making space for such negotiation in doctoral progress reporting or assessment work.

Researcher developers can influence departments to encourage supervisors to create regular opportunities for discussion of key elements of students' desired repertoires and to use well-judged questions to help students engage more deeply, 'owning' answers which are plausible to them, and contributing to deeper learning. This ownership might involve helping supervisors develop cultures of principled self- and peer-assessment.

More challengingly, researcher developers could facilitate supervisors' understanding of the value of critical inclusion activities such as co-writing with doctoral students, and involving students as critical friends on supervisors' own work in progress.

Many doctoral supervisors already engage in similar supervisory practices. Exploring and sharing such collegial, decentring practices can help departments embed this way of developing researchers.

David Hyatt

Complementary ideas include **18**, **24** and **44**.

20 The imposter syndrome in researchers

About 70 per cent of people across all genders occasionally experience imposter feelings and about 30 per cent of people have persistent imposter feelings – the imposter syndrome.

Imposter feelings
These are occasional feelings of having misrepresented yourself, despite there being clear evidence to the contrary; sometimes feeling like you don't deserve to be where you are, or that you will be 'found out'.

Imposter syndrome
Imposter syndrome is a persistent set of thoughts, feelings and behaviours that result from the perception of having misrepresented yourself, despite clear evidence to the contrary; feeling like an imposter a lot of the time in a way that affects what you think, feel and do.

How does the imposter syndrome impact on the work of researcher developers?
The research environment can foster imposter feelings. It attracts high-achieving people who are often perfectionist, there are regular setbacks and their outputs are subject to intense scrutiny and often harsh criticism. These people need our support. And researcher developers can experience it too! We often have to prove our credibility and show how what we do makes a difference too.

Strategies for combating imposter feelings
One of the characteristics of imposter feelings/syndrome is that they are kept secret. Naturally enough we don't want to be found out as a fraud. Yet at least 70 per cent of people do experience

imposter feelings. So naming and normalising these feelings is the most effective strategy. A short workshop session of 30–60 minutes could touch on the topics below:

1) Introduce the concepts of imposter feelings/syndrome.
2) Provide examples of when participants may feel like an imposter, e.g. starting a new project, writing a paper, giving a conference presentation.
3) Discuss your own experiences of imposter feelings.
4) Get a senior researcher or experienced doctoral researcher to talk about their imposter feelings and how they respond. Or organise a panel to discuss their experiences.
5) Provide time for small group discussions. Realising that their peers feel similarly is very powerful. Don't push people to reveal or discuss more than they feel comfortable with.
6) Offer specific strategies.
7) Remembering that it's normal.
8) Look at the facts. Even though participants might feel like an imposter the facts show that they are not.
9) Manage the feelings. They don't go away. But take action anyway.
10) Provide resources, e.g. handouts.

The session length depends on how much discussion and question time is needed. It could be built into researcher induction/orientation as a 30-minute session. When researchers begin a new role they are very likely to doubt themselves, and it's reassuring to realise that this is normal and most people feel the same way. A shortened version could be incorporated into other workshops, seminar series, mentoring programmes or community spaces.

Supervisor development
Sessions as suggested above could be included in supervisor development programmes too. Supervisors can then recognise and discuss these ideas with their doctoral researchers and research staff.

When to refer

These strategies will help for imposter feelings. However, the imposter syndrome involves more embedded or strongly-held beliefs, and the researcher may need further specialist support. Here it is important for us as researcher developers to realise that we are not therapists and be clear about our professional boundaries. So at this point refer the researcher to other support such as counselling services.

A free resource on imposter syndrome is available at impostersyndrome.com.au/index.php/the-free-guide/

Hugh Kearns

Complementary ideas include **17**, **21** and **24**.

Chapter 4
Developing effective communicators

21 Academic writing: it's more than a matter of brainpower

There is more to writing than skill, subject knowledge and ability. The 'affective', in other words the feeling and emotional side of writing – enjoyment, motivation, drive, passion, enthusiasm, inspiration – has a strong influence.

I believe proper attention should be paid to the affective side of researcher writing. We all know from experience that writing involves a great deal of cognitive energy. It makes your brain hurt. But for most people, writing is also an experience that involves strong feelings and emotions: pain; pleasure; fear; frustration; enjoyment; angst; annoyance; relief; and stress.

What do researchers say about the affective side of writing?

Based on my own research and supervision of writing, I summarise here the main positive and negative views and feelings that writers express. First, some positive viewpoints and attitudes:

- Writing develops ideas and arguments, it clarifies and organises thoughts.
- Writing is part of learning, processing and thinking.
- Writing is catharsis: 'getting it out', and making thoughts tangible.
- Writing leads to feelings of achievement, pride and even elation.

When researchers are asked to reflect on their negative feelings towards writing they express a variety of sentiments: feelings of frustration and 'hard work'; the common difficulty of 'getting started'; feelings of pressure, fear and anxiety, such as 'I feel pressure to be "correct"'. There are other feelings of stress relating to 'knowing the rules of the game', for example: 'Will I, or must I, be too conformist?' 'Do I have to stick to the rules?'

Negative feelings lead to barriers and blocks to student writing
For example:

- When we feel insecure, we're not convinced of the direction we are going in – are we including the right things?
- Thinking is non-linear, everything is connected, but our writing has to be a linear story, with a beginning and an end. Where to start?
- Wanting to be concise, and make a clear point, and knowing that we can ramble on;
- Striving for 'perfect' and trying to produce writing in a format and to a standard that will please others.

Mental clutter, and emotional fatigue in our day-to-day lives are often cited as writing barriers: moods; family; job; not being able to concentrate; time management; and other obligations. Additionally, interactions between supervisor and student can generate barrier emotions: 'There seems to be an understanding gap between me and my supervisor' or 'Comments from my supervisor sometimes immobilise me.' So you can see that in order to write well and enjoy writing, it's worth considering what's going on emotionally.

How can researcher developers help writers?
Practical points emerge in reflecting on emotional barriers. First, this aspect of writing is extremely important to researchers – they talk about it with some enthusiasm and humour. Researchers have many positive attitudes and feelings about writing that are well worth celebrating, sharing, and building upon through development activities.

Secondly, having time and permission to open up, reflect and share with fellow writers is a vitally important one – not only to make writers 'feel better', but also as a starting point to help them evaluate and improve their own writing practices. Many researchers are able to gain perspective on their writing, and plan around difficulties as a result of unburdening and discussion in small groups.

Lastly, we do not see such reflections and confessions about being stuck with writing as weakness or low competence. The act of admitting being stuck and evaluating why is a positive one, it is an important part of self-reflection and a feature of the criticality that we hope to develop in higher education and the research environment.

Jerry Wellington

Complementary ideas include **17**, **22**, **23** and **24**.

22 Techniques to encourage early and frequent writing

People in universities complain about writing. I have heard colleagues describe it as a chore and students a burden, a time-consuming and anxious task typically performed under the pressure of deadlines. At the same time, many researchers also believe the writing process could be beneficial, even creative, if only they had more time, confidence or ability. It is the task of the researcher developer to help researchers to structure writing time and cultivate writing confidence in order to reinforce this latent belief.

The inner critic

You must help writers to censor the inner critic with habit. There is a freedom in the acceptance of mistakes. A daily writing habit (even 20 minutes) is beneficial and liberating, because quality then becomes less important than the act of writing itself. It doesn't matter what people write, or how 'good' it is, just that they write regularly to set targets.

There are plenty of websites that facilitate writing routines and you should familiarise yourself with them.

An example schedule: daily writing for 30 minutes to an achievable word count, Monday–Friday, for a week. Then take a week off. Then try a fortnight of the same schedule, with a week off, scale until the researcher is writing for four out of every five weeks. That's a writing habit.

I begin by editing what I have written the day before, tinkering until I am ready to go. Revision is part of the process, and there is nothing wrong with getting rid of previous work. Build in time off: once a section or a chapter is complete, encourage researchers to take a break and then come back to edit.

My mind goes blank

When in doubt, freewrite. Run a workshop with researchers where you time them for one to ten minutes and ask them to write at pace, not stopping till the timer ends, even if they think they're writing nonsense. Explain that this will, at the least, produce text to edit or delete later, and at best provide insight.

Once they are comfortable with this, introduce the clustering technique: each writes a title or key phrase in the centre of their page and then spins out words or phrases, following chains of association from the centre. This helps map out the territory for freewriting. Try factoring in three minutes' clustering, three minutes' freewriting and three minutes' editing. Post-workshop opportunities to reflect and cement the learning will also help them.

Writing about writing

The more we appreciate how words construct personas (like the rigorous expert or the organised facilitator) the more we understand how our writing can work against us, dictating how we present things. To help researchers understand, encourage personal reflective writing. This can help them find a voice, a way of writing that connects their words to the person writing them.

Give out notebooks and ask researchers to make observations about previous work in comparison with current. Encourage them to write in the first person, thinking about what they wrote and are trying to do. Bring researchers together to share observations from their notebooks.

Final words

Writing is a process that works best when researchers invest in daily habits using productive techniques like freewriting, regular editing and reflection. Your role is to make this happen. Ask researchers to commit to a writing club. Freewrite together every time you meet, discuss observations and share best practice at keeping to the rhythms of a writing habit. Peer critique between group members will lead to further revision. Celebrate publications and achievements, invite new members and keep it going!

Matthew Cheeseman

Complementary ideas include **21**.

23 Individual writing advice

Offering individual writing advice for doctoral researchers
Individual writing advice helps doctoral researchers, both home and international, *learn* about writing and recognise what they need to build upon. Doctoral researchers enter their studies with mixed writing abilities and although many supervisors often advise their students with their writing, it is not always a focus and not all supervisors are good writers. Writing advice for doctoral researchers has been offered at Royal Holloway, University of London for two years and requests for advice have been increasing.

Content of individual writing advice
Practically, individual sessions usually take about an hour and reading the draft beforehand can take anything from one to three hours. There is a broad range of writing ability at PhD level and so while some doctoral researchers require advice on language and grammar, others will need help with style, clarity and voice. Discussions about writing can help doctoral researchers articulate their aims, and a non-specialist view of their literature review can help them craft their own voice amongst that of their disciplinary peers.

As it is not a proofreading service only short sections are read in depth – looking for recurring and consistent errors – and then the rest is scanned for structural issues.

Writing advice can help doctoral researchers deal with issues such as writing block and writing aversion. I've found that blocks can occur when they feel isolated or come up against obstacles in their research and often they do not want to admit to their supervisor that they are struggling or writing too little. Talking through their ideas with someone who is not a specialist in their subject can help to alleviate this.

Outcomes

Writing advice gives doctoral researchers the chance to discuss their research without pressures or expectations and if started early on in their studies can have a meaningful effect on their literacy and writing style. Feedback from doctoral researchers who have attended individual advice sessions say that they feel more motivated to write, that they feel more equipped to approach writing differently and more effectively, and in some instances it has changed the way they view their work. Doctoral researchers have felt more empowered to ask for explanations to questions they were too embarrassed to ask their supervisor. Individual writing advice can help to develop a doctoral researcher's confidence and encourages them to take a reflexive view of their writing.

Advising doctoral researchers with their drafts before they submit them to their supervisors can mean that these meetings then focus on the complexities of the research and not the surface errors or on deeper writing issues. Therefore, in quantitative terms, individual writing advice offers value for money.

Future of individual writing advice

Regular meetings have helped the productivity of some doctoral researchers and in this sense helped to create a writing habit, which is often the key to completion.

Common writing issues that are noticed in advice sessions can be used as a basis for further discussion in supervisor development courses.

Laura Christie

Complementary ideas include **2** and **22**.

24 Thesis mentoring: busting myths and assumptions in doctoral writing

Barriers to thesis writing, and all academic writing, can stem from emotional or motivational roots. Some doctoral students are overwhelmed by writing and feelings of guilt and shame about the doctorate. In a profession where self-worth is influenced by academic performance, thesis writing can trigger significant fear-based delay or avoidance tactics.

The Thesis Mentoring Programme

The Thesis Mentoring Programme at The University of Sheffield, UK, was designed using three drivers in the development of doctoral writers:

1) Feelings of inadequacy as writers. Students struggling to write, or start writing, can perceive this to result from a deficit in innate writing ability, rather than a lack of practice. This false 'capable–incapable student' dichotomy is sometimes perpetuated by supervisors too – unhelpfully, as the context and working relationships of the writer influence writing performance. The confidence to take ownership of challenging tasks, and succeed, is dependent on how well supported writers feel in their endeavour, and the quality of the feedback they receive on their achievements.

2) The 'writing up is supposed to be hard' myth. The doctorate is often unhelpfully cut into a data/analysis phase, and a writing-up phase. As writing begins, messages that 'it's supposed to be hard', or, 'it's a rite of passage' can make writers fearful, which leads to avoidance and a sense of powerlessness about changing or managing the experience.

3) The intent to formalise and document the unrecognised supervisory support that postdoctoral research staff provide

to thesis writers informally. Furthermore, to deliver writing-support skills development to postdoctoral staff, who are the next generation of research supervisors.

Programme design

The Thesis Mentoring Programme takes an 'assumption-busting' position, and enables incremental, practice-based development towards completion, through coaching conversations. It views:

- writing as a practice, not innate ability, or a skill set;
- writing as a way of thinking, not a means of recording;
- writing as a process – you can't know it all before you start.

The programme uses a solutions-focused coaching approach, assuming no deficit in the writer, and posits that to progress the writer must reframe their thinking about themselves and the practice and process of writing. It places emphasis on doing more of what works for each writer, and doing less of what does not. It signposts to support from others, including specialist support teams and most importantly, the student's own supervisor(s).

Following mentor and mentee group inductions, objective setting, and matching, one-to-one sessions commence (eight one-hour meetings over 16 weeks). Explicit role definitions enable complementarity in the doctoral student's sources of support, and protect the mentor from getting into the conflict territory of advising on thesis content. The mentor is not a substitute supervisor; their role is to provide an objective viewpoint to help the student develop good writing practices. For this reason mentor–mentee pairs are always from different disciplines.

Data collation and results

Data are collated from mentee application forms, group discussions, and programme evaluations and show that writing anxieties are contextual and are inextricable from the writer's research environment and supervisory relationship(s). However, students are able to find ways to overcome their writing barriers when given the opportunity to reflect and discuss, and once a student has been able to solve a problem they gain confidence in their writing and their ability to finish the doctorate. Encouragingly, even students who experience a total breakdown in communication with their supervisor find it possible to renegotiate a working relationship. Mentors reported that the programme helps them to develop a more considered and reflective approach to supervision and a greater understanding of the issues of thesis writers.

Kay Guccione

Complementary ideas include **17**, **20**, **21** and **26**.

Thesis mentoring **24**

25 Partnering with actors to enhance researcher development workshops

Researcher development professionals know from experience that when developing presentation skills in a workshop, participants benefit from both personal feedback on their own performances, and the opportunity to observe the presentation styles of others. Local professional actors make great partners in enhancing learning in a Presentation Skills Masterclass.

Workshop design
Due to both the time constraints and participant fear factor in our previous (small-group feedback) workshop design, we had to think creatively about how to maximise learning for our researchers.

In advance of the workshop, we helped participants to video record ten-minute research presentations (attended by a small group of friends and lab colleagues). We then provided individual feedback on their performance as the opening to the subsequent one-day workshop.

Involving local actors to demonstrate particular presentation styles allowed group discussion around presentation characteristics, presenter styles, and the impact of these on the audience.

We recruited actors through local professional acting networks, providing them with a character brief and accompanying presentation slides. The detailed brief included behaviour cues that created caricatures of two common 'ineffective' presentation styles. We briefed the actors to ensure familiarisation with terminology, so they would be convincing as 'real researchers' at the university.

On the day

The two actors 'in character' join the workshop over lunch and are introduced to the participants as researchers who have been invited to share how they present.

Character 1: A nervous PhD student who arrives looking terrified, struggles to eat and pores over their notes. They panic about how the technology works, and who the audience is. During their presentation they:

- apologise repeatedly for their presentation;
- speak too quietly; the voice is strained due to nerves;
- read from notes, holding them in front of their face;
- use repeated nervous and jittery hand gestures;
- get upset when the notes and slides are not as expected;
- make excuses for presentation: *My supervisor told me to do it, I don't know why.*

Character 2: An arrogant senior researcher, who is rude to the workshop facilitator and complains loudly about the facilities, lunch, technology, etc. They spend the lunch break on the phone talking rudely to a colleague who needs their help. During this presentation they:

- have too much information on the slides, which they read out;
- speak quickly in a bored, patronising and mechanical way;
- use too many slide animations, get annoyed and blame the technology;
- use phrases like: *You'll have to trust me on that; I'm not explaining that; If you don't know what this is then there's no point going on;*
- have far too many slides, and have to be stopped at the time limit. They angrily blame the facilitator.

Value added

'Watching the actors give examples of poor presentations was interesting and useful, especially after the brainstorming session on what makes a bad presentation.'

The components of ineffective presentations are clearly demonstrated to the participants in this way and the audience really gets to feel the impact of certain behaviours. Not all participants will realise the presenters are actors until it is revealed. There is also the added benefit of a group Q&A with actors on their top tips for preparing for and dealing with public speaking: 'Observing the actors giving bad presentations and discussion from the audience perspective was an eye opener.'

An additional learning point is how participants formulate opinions of the two characters over lunch. First impressions count at conferences, and this powerfully demonstrates how perceptions outside the presentation itself do matter: 'The actors were brilliant, the rudeness over lunch was very convincing!'

Lucy Lee, Robert Myles and Kay Guccione

Complementary ideas include **5**.

Chapter 5
Peer learning and support

26 Critical career evaluation for research staff – a mentoring programme design

Conversations with research staff about their career progression revealed a clear gap for meaningful 'critical conversations' with senior colleagues, and prompted a bespoke mentoring programme design at The University of Sheffield, UK. The resulting programme is open to all staff who consider themselves to be active in research and provides access to outsider opinions that aid development and career planning.

Typically participants are (postdoctoral) research associates, assistants, fellows and new lecturers, but may also include staff in other roles who are developing research practices. Participants number around 150 annually across two six-month programmes. The mentor pool (150+), are academic volunteers, trained in mentoring and coaching. The programme is driven by the mentees and they take the lead for mentoring. Mentee engagement is not limited to those aiming to progress into academic posts. Researchers who want to consider wider career options represent the largest group of mentees.

All mentors and mentees attend an induction workshop that sets expectations for mentoring roles, boundaries and relationship dynamics. Afterwards, participants complete a form that allows the programme manager to match suitable pairs. Experience shows that sustained success is more than a product of simply matching two people together to transfer know-how, and some underpinning ideas are highlighted below.

1. What's the institutional reputation of mentoring?
Listen to how people talk about mentoring and work with these messages. It will help you design something with reassurances built in.

2. Create a mentor role complementary to the role of the principal investigator

It's important that the mentor is not a substitute line manager. This can create role conflict, and pressure on the mentor to 'manage' the mentee. A space for honest, open discussions is more easily cultivated if the mentee and mentor are from different departments.

3. Start small

You only need five to ten pairs for a pilot. Remember that the mentees will leave but well looked-after mentors remain for re-matching. Take care of the mentors and they will deliver researcher development for you.

4. Be clear about expectations, responsibilities, and who drives

Is your programme more about advising, or more about coaching? There's room for interpretation in mentoring roles, and clashed assumptions can end a partnership. Mentee development is their own responsibility; they make contact, set objectives and feedback.

5. Give them a 'get out'

Let people who hated the induction leave, offer a 'no blame divorce' clause in case of mismatches, create a time limit to the partnerships (that does not exclude short fixed-term contracts) and expect them to end there. Though, of course, staying paired is a positive outcome.

6. Tailor the programme

Do your aims align with real researcher issues? An evidence-based approach works well; what's in the literature to support your programme's design? Be aware that a coaching style is in tension with normal academic modes of advising and consulting. Encourage mentors to consider this and find their own style.

7. Matching is an art

Matching processes benefit from asking participants' likes as well as career barriers and aspirations. Matching for 'something similar' means they will find common ground; adding 'something different' affords new learning. Tell each pair why they have been matched together.

8. Listen to the participants
Programme evaluation data will give you insight into the mentoring outcomes, but also inform you on what the participants didn't know about, found confusing, or hated. Add questions on – and listen out for – areas to develop.

Kay Guccione

Complementary ideas include **2**, **24** and **27**.

27 How sponsorship develops capability from mentoring relationships

From mentoring to sponsorship

Mentoring of a junior research colleague by someone more senior or experienced is seen to be an effective part of career development whether it happens informally between colleagues or more formally across a department, faculty, institution or discipline.

The opportunity to transfer knowledge, experience, guidance and opinion differentiates mentoring from coaching or counselling. It is often a two-way process, since mentors learn as much about the status quo and barriers to progression at more junior levels from their mentee as mentees learn about promotion, politics and navigating the environment from their mentor.

So far, so familiar.

But what of sponsorship? Sponsorship takes mentoring a stage further. Here, the more senior person gives the junior colleague an opportunity they wouldn't previously have had, by means of, say, a personal recommendation or an introduction to a colleague that opens a networking opportunity.

Sponsorship may happen naturally in all organisations when a senior researcher, for instance, makes a recommendation that a more junior colleague should take up a specific committee role, be invited to be a speaker at an event or be put forward for a promotion. This sponsorship does not necessarily involve the precursor of mentoring but it almost always relies upon the more junior person being recognised as being suitable for the opportunity, having a profile with those more senior and 'being known' for what they do or have the potential to contribute. Often researchers can be reluctant to promote their achievements and capabilities and so there can sometimes only be a small number of people who are selected for such sponsorship in relation to the overall pool of available candidates. Sponsorship schemes are about increasing the total number of junior people whose skills and abilities are known within an environment.

The process

The School of Sport, Exercise and Health Sciences at Loughborough University, UK, wanted to develop a supportive programme for a mixed-gender group of researchers in first or second academic posts within the School. The notion that a sponsorship relationship should emerge from mentoring was explicit for all applicants. Mentors were approached on the basis of their existing supportive behaviours for those that they line managed, mentored already and supervised.

Initially, mentees were paired with a more senior male or female mentor from within the School outside their individual discipline area. Over a 12-month period the programme started with a researcher developer-led workshop for each cohort to explore opportunities, challenges and sources of support. Creating a mentor–mentee relationship through one-to-one meetings initiated the programme. As the mentor became the sponsor they were asked to look out for and create opportunities that would benefit both the mentee and the recommended situation and crucially for which the mentee was ready but may not have had the opportunity to put themselves forward for. Sponsorship activities included: help in development of individual research strategies; building and developing the researcher's profile in their subject and within the University; helping to review CV and applications ahead of promotion deadlines; and encouraging engagement in committee and structured work within the School and University.

The future

The aim of this programme is ultimately to improve the quality and diversity of the School's leaders at every level. Twelve months from the start, the majority of mentoring relationships initiated had developed into fledgling sponsorship opportunities. Relationships developed at different rates and there were early opportunities to help, introduce and recommend for some.

What makes this mentoring programme different is that there is an explicit understanding right from the start that creating and taking opportunities is part of the mutual contract between sponsor/mentor and mentee. This is built into both expectation and design at the start and it must work on the basis of mutual trust and moving at the right pace, as well as the sponsor considering that small actions they might make can have an exponentially bigger effect for the mentee.

Fehmidah Munir and Janet Wilkinson

Complementary ideas include **2**, **19** and **26**.

28 Mentoring for doctoral researchers

Creating a mentoring scheme for doctoral researchers

At Royal Holloway, University of London, we set up a scheme whereby doctoral researchers were mentored by early career research staff. Mentors would: help ease intellectual isolation; provide motivation and advice with career and skills development goals; talk through difficulties with research and/or writing; be part of a friendly support network for doctoral researchers in addition to a supervisor. In our scheme, a mentor plays a distinct role outside of the supervisory team and is not a substitute for the supervisor.

Setting up a mentoring scheme

Setting up the scheme required very little administrative time. To make it attractive to research staff we highlighted the benefits such as using this experience as evidence for promotion criteria. It can also be used for Higher Education Academy recognition as evidence of leadership and influence for Senior Fellowship applications through institutional continuing professional development (CPD) schemes or the independent route.

We sent out individual invitations to selected research staff, which proved to be more effective than one mass email, particularly if someone in their department had provided a personal recommendation. When we considered how long mentoring relationships should last and how many meetings we should recommend during this time, we concluded that a one-year relationship with a minimum of four meetings during this period should provide enough time for both mentor and mentee to see meaningful progress. We decided to match the mentor and mentee from different departments so that the focus of the mentoring would be the doctoral researcher's skills and career development and not discussions of their research.

We kept the application form simple so that matching would not be too complicated, and therefore did not ask focused questions. Supervisors were asked to support their student's application for a mentor so that the relationship is transparent and supervisors know their students are receiving career and development advice from a mentor.

We recommended that mentor and mentee discuss an informal contract (provided) at the initial meeting, to help to establish expectations from the outset. Points for them to consider were: to agree on how many times to meet; where to meet; how progress is documented; and who will be responsible for keeping records of the meeting. We recommended to research staff that they ask their mentee to write a summary of each meeting and send it to the mentor for approval to avoid miscommunications.

Outcomes
Expectations from a couple of doctoral researchers were too focused and this led to unsuccessful matches, so we tried to keep expectations of the scheme clear.

Mid-year feedback from doctoral researchers in the first year of running the scheme indicated that having a mentor has encouraged them to start planning their next steps after the PhD, and facilitates helpful discussions on other issues, such as bridging the gap between study and work. Doctoral researchers said they appreciated discussing these issues with someone outside their department and have on the whole felt encouraged, while supervisors have supported the mentoring scheme and some have encouraged their students to apply.

Laura Christie

Complementary ideas include **24**.

Chapter 6
Development through external experiences

29 Engagement beyond the ivory tower

Researchers have lately been bombarded by demands for 'public engagement' and 'outreach' activity. It is expected unilaterally that researchers should be effective communicators. Television schedules are now incomplete without documentaries presented by a slick academic with a reassuring, credible manner. Research in general is becoming accountability-driven and – immaterial of funding stream – must show value in order to ensure continued financial underpinning. This means researchers have to venture outside their ivory towers. So, what can we do to help them prepare for public engagement activity?

What are the options?
Often, initiatives exist already. The UK has for some years had national schemes such as Researchers in Residence (researchers spending time in schools to enthuse pupils and enhance the curriculum) that individual institutions have now adopted, and which provide excellent development activities. Plus, engagement initiatives that provide formal training (such as those organised by Wellcome and the Arts Council) grow year on year. If you are a researcher developer looking to enhance your development programmes with external opportunities, or to adapt these ideas to run in-house, the UK National Coordinating Centre for Public Engagement (www. publicengagement.ac.uk) provides a comprehensive base for ideas and good practice.

But before any activity is undertaken, we should also offer help in identifying exactly a) the *purpose* of the activity, and b) who the prospective *audience* might be. Our sector is somewhat lax in this regard. For instance, the terms 'public engagement' and 'outreach' are often erroneously used interchangeably; and indeed the labels imply that the 'public' is a homogenous entity rather than diverse sub-groups.

Our next role is to provide information about opportunities. Listed here are some current initiatives that could be adopted in an institutional portfolio:

Three Minute Thesis
Developed by the University of Queensland, Australia, now widely adopted, 3MT® asks researchers to explain their work concisely to non-specialists (threeminutethesis.org).

FameLab
This is an international communications competition that engages and entertains by illustrating academic concepts in short presentations (famelab.org).

Stand-up comedy
Daunting but both empowering and entertaining: search for Bright Club – a national UK initiative (brightclub.org).

Dance Your Ph.D.
Combining academic and artistic merit, this competition attracts international research entries (gonzolabs.org/dance).

Cafe Scientifique
Researchers contribute to academic-themed public debates in venues outside of a typical academic context (cafescientifique.org).

STEM for BRITAIN
A poster event (setforbritain.org.uk/) to facilitate the exchange of ideas between research and government (formerly SET for BRITAIN). Its overall aim is to encourage, support and promote Britain's early-stage and early-career researchers in the STEM disciplines: science, engineering, technology and mathematics.

I'm a Scientist
I'm a Scientist, Get Me Out of Here is an online event where schools interact with and judge researchers in a TV-style talent competition (imascientist.org.uk/).

Soapbox Science
Soapbox Science promotes women scientists and their research by converting public areas into learning and debate forums (soapboxscience.org/).

British Science Association
BSA is an organisation that aims to support and grow the communication of science and research. Their annual festival offers many opportunities (britishscienceassociation.org/).

STEMNET
The Science, Technology, Engineering and Mathematics Network provides opportunities for researchers to become ambassadors to inspire young people in these subject areas (stemnet.org.uk/).

Getting the most out of engagement

Regardless of the initiative or scheme, the key to developmental activity is to balance support and challenge. For many researchers, the act of performing comedy or dance might be challenging enough even without a research element, and it is here that confidence coaching might be needed. For others, it may be less a confidence issue and more about knowing how to simplify their message – in this case, workshops may be beneficial.

In order to ensure a full learning experience, we must help researchers articulate why they want to get involved in engagement and develop a palatable rationale for how these activities can add value to their departmental research outputs. After all, these initiatives are all potentially valuable, but they do take away time from the production of research outputs – and as such can be opposed by some academics.

Additionally, researcher developers must provide a forum for the researchers to reflect upon and articulate the value of their activities. How did it make them better researchers? What *lessons* were learned? What *insights* did the process give them for their research? And how can they articulate this in funding applications or reporting?

Ultimately, there are dozens of engagement schemes available, and many offer bespoke training. So we must let people know what is available, provide the support they need to perform at their best, and help them to reflect upon and articulate the value that was gained. This value is, of course, to the myriad 'publics', to the institution, but above all to the field of research and the researchers themselves.

Steve Hutchinson

Complementary ideas include **31** and **40**.

30 Creating effective structures for doctoral internships

That the majority of doctoral graduates do not pursue an academic career has sharpened our focus on employability. Pressure for universities to work with businesses has encouraged us to look outward. A successful doctoral internship (DI) programme may help us in both of these endeavours.

Prerequisites for a successful programme
For a DI programme to be successful we need four things:

1) *A clear, fair and inclusive procedure.* Limiting DIs to a small minority of researchers isn't going to help us meet our obligations towards employability and partner engagement. We need to:
   - clarify our stance on unpaid DIs, stipend arrangements, funding for travel and accommodation;
   - consider how DIs can be made available to international researchers without contravening any visa restrictions;
   - define practicalities (e.g. when DIs take place) and processes for vetting organisations, projects and locations.

2) *Align DIs with research success measures.* Academic staff are measured on research income and outputs, and successful doctoral completions, and penalised if researchers do not finish on time. To reduce the likelihood of an internship having a negative impact on research outputs and timely thesis submission, its length and format should be considered. It may be beneficial for an internship to take place two days a week over a longer time period. For DIs that are longer, it may be possible to consider a leave of absence (LOA), although this arrangement is not without its issues – this option is not possible for international researchers and is also incompatible with the ethos of the internship as a valued component of the study.

3) *Source meaningful and appropriate internships.* Meaningful internships must meet the researcher's learning objectives (e.g. exploring career paths or finding collaborative partners for subsequent research proposals). There must be a way of identifying and communicating with suitable organisations, or supporting researchers to do so. Organisations may be unfamiliar with the researcher skillset and experience, and unclear about the doctoral timeframe, for example by assuming that doctoral internships, like many undergraduate internships, take place in the long vacation.

4) *Sufficient resources.* Managing internships is resource intensive. It requires dedicated staff, and systems that track and report data (health and safety documentation, induction processes, learning objectives, personal details, outcomes and impact).

Our approach
The Careers Service at The University of Sheffield, UK, created a Placement Team with a remit to promote and administer placements across the entire university. By enrolling onto a formal DI module, the researcher is supported through the whole process and can, through assessment records, evidence that the internship is an integral and valuable part of their study. Researchers can apply to a DI hardship fund to support significant additional costs such as travel and accommodation.

UK research councils demand that 70 per cent of doctorates that they fund are submitted on time, and we are exploring ways in which DIs might be incorporated without threatening the submission rate. The White Rose College of the Arts & Humanities, UK, (wrocah.ac.uk) offers post-DI researchers an additional month of funding (after thesis submission) for paper writing.

Each university will have different tools for addressing the challenges, according to institutional strengths, partners, objectives and organisational structure. Most will have existing expertise and resources (e.g. undergraduate placements) that can be adapted.

Despite these challenges, DIs are a hugely beneficial adjunct to the doctorate, and should be pursued. At Sheffield, proactive work in establishing internships has led to new relationships between the University and hosting organisations. My own research has shown that post-DI supervisors benefit from more mature, motivated and skilled researchers, keen to submit and take the next steps in their careers. Concerns about loss of focus or falling behind were largely unsubstantiated: the fear of this was much worse than the reality.

Hilary Jones

Complementary ideas include **32**.

31 Charity Stretch: value-added learning and development from real-life projects

Researcher developers are accustomed to using experiential development exercises where participants are given a 'case study' – a situation-based problem – which they need to solve. These exercises are often very effective, though frequently criticised by participants on the grounds that they are not 'real'. This line is sometimes used by participants to excuse their lack of engagement in areas of personal development that they identify but which are perhaps difficult or unpleasant. This problem inspired the idea for Charity Stretch.

Charity Stretch is learning based around a real project. The aim is for a group of participants to organise a real event to raise real money for a real charitable organisation of the participants' choice. The role of the researcher developer is to observe, to stand alongside the participants as they work together, to provide coaching when required, and – crucially – to debrief the results and thus maximise the learning. The intervention's name relates to the fact it has a dual purpose: to benefit a charity; and to stretch the participants' potential.

The process
A Charity Stretch programme lasts up to three months, becoming less structured as time goes on. In our experience, the following process worked well:

An initial introductory session
This outlined the project, and provided space for a crucial values-based discussion, which was central to the purpose of Charity Stretch. In the same way that individuals make decisions as to which charitable causes to support financially based on their values, so the group decision of which organisation to support

needed to be based on individuals identifying and sharing their values, then coming to a consensus on what was important.

A session on project management
In addition to outlining general principles, this session provided a focused opportunity for participants to begin to actively manage their event as a group project. In a facilitated discussion, participants were encouraged to articulate the key aims of their project and a deadline to which they would work (with interim targets). Responsibilities were also assigned to each group member. This provided a framework by which groups could review their progress at frequent intervals.

Preparation and planning
This phase was the responsibility of the groups. The facilitator met with them at least twice to monitor progress and allow group issues to be aired.

The main event
Charity Stretch events have included an art auction that raised over five thousand pounds, a campus-based weekend lunch event that raised several hundred pounds, and a fashion show in aid of an Armed Forces charity.

Post-event review
This is where the success of the event was celebrated and the learning from the process distilled. A facilitated discussion allowed the participants to share their perspectives on what went well, what they each individually did to create that success and what could have been improved upon. This is where the value of the project from a learning perspective came to the fore.

Each part of Charity Stretch has development potential: from the choice of beneficiary charity, allowing participants to articulate their values, through the planning and execution of the event itself, with all the project management skills that involves. Throughout the project, group work allows opportunities for development of leadership and negotiation skills. Many development projects offer similar opportunities; the real impact of Charity Stretch is in the authenticity of the project. The stakes are high for all concerned, resulting in the most transformative of experiences.

Helen Lawrence

Complementary ideas include **32** and **43**.

32 The benefits to researchers of working on consultancy projects

Researchers today are under pressure to share their research with the wider world. We know we need to show the impact of our research and that public engagement is crucial to success, but how can we do that when research so often seems obscure to others? And how can we help new researchers develop the high-level skills they need to succeed – either in this new research environment or, increasingly, in the world outside academia? Placements can be problematic: often researchers feel exploited by being given menial tasks, and organisations feel researchers aren't properly engaging with the work. One answer is to focus more on consultancy, with short projects, agreed with partner organisations, managed by individual researchers, with tangible outcomes. This is how you do it, using a real-life example.

Develop short projects
The main point here is that it's not your project. You invite an organisation to identify something they wish to achieve, and work with them to develop a brief that's achievable in a short timescale. Three to five days is ideal, and this can be in one block or spread over several weeks. Researchers then apply to work on the project, and, once accepted, agree the details of how to do it with the organisations. For example, a local museum, though initially sceptical that anything useful could be achieved, was persuaded to suspend their disbelief and develop a brief to revamp its ceramics gallery, which was dated and tired-looking, and didn't attract many visitors. The brief was to find out what people would really like to see. The researcher who worked on the project, Amy, didn't think a traditional survey would tell them anything useful, and used a different approach based on her own research methodology.

The researcher manages the project

Researchers need to bear two things in mind. Firstly, the project or organisation needn't necessarily be directly related to their research topic. The purpose of the exercise is to engage with a non-academic organisation using generic, professional skills like communication, project management and collaborative working. Secondly, what they bring to the project is research knowledge and expertise, which can be brought to bear on a variety of situations. The researcher must develop the approach, sell it to the organisation, then manage it to fruition.

Amy welcomed the opportunity to adapt her own creative methodology in the museum project to develop what she called the 'curation game'. This involved presenting a number of objects, representing objects in the collection, and inviting people to choose from these to make their own display. The display was photographed and Amy asked them for their thoughts on it. The whole project, including meetings with the museum, developing the game, consultation, and final report, took the equivalent of five days, providing Amy with professional experience in a wider context.

Have a tangible outcome

Having a tangible outcome gives the project credibility; for the partner organisation, for your institution, and for the researcher. This can be a presentation, a report, or a set of recommendations. Amy produced a report with recommendations for the gallery, which the museum incorporated into their plans.

You might think this kind of scheme is challenging – and it is. Organisations initially have to be persuaded that something useful can be done in a few days, and researchers have to be convinced that they don't *have* to work just within their own narrow topic. But once persuaded, researchers find it hugely rewarding, and organisations are often so impressed they come back for more.

Anne Boultwood

Complementary ideas include **30**, **31** and **41**.

Chapter 7
Supporting career development

33 Creating career stories for research staff career development

Introduction
Career development often comes low on a researcher's list of priorities, yet exploring the reality of a career in academia or the skills required to move onto an alternative pathway is key to career progression. Well produced, accessible and honest case studies can inspire researchers to explore their career options and engage with career development opportunities. Such career stories need to resonate with a wide range of researchers, independent of their career stage and their discipline.

Identifying the team
The skills and experience required to create a good set of career stories is unlikely to be found in a single individual. It is likely that a small team will be required to successfully complete such a project. Team roles may include researcher developer, graphic designer, web developer, publicity officer and researchers themselves. Once identified, it is worth ensuring all the team are clear on the aim of the project and that they are clear on their role within it. Getting the team to meet early and regularly will help to ensure the project maintains momentum.

Creating the resource
There are two principal aspects to creating career stories: firstly, collecting the stories; and secondly, translating these into a useful resource.

Planning and collecting
In order to identify which career stories will be most appropriate you will need a clear understanding of the intended audience. Will the audience be within a single discipline or from a wide range of disciplines? Will they be at similar career stages? Once identified, you can then select individuals who will resonate

with this audience and inspire them to engage with their career development. It is often useful to speak with a sample of the intended audience to identify the information important to them. This will help to ensure that your resource is beneficial, relevant and ultimately valuable to your audience.

Another important consideration is how many career stories to produce. Less is more: too many case studies may mean your project loses focus. A dozen carefully chosen examples should give you sufficient breadth of careers and give you enough time to create a quality resource.

Deciding what information you need and how to collect it are significant challenges. You may draw upon a number of sources such as CVs, interviews, questionnaires or online profiles. Depth and quality will be gained by working with the individuals in your stories to refine this information.

Producing the resource
Deciding on format(s) is another important consideration. Printed media can be restrictive, but many researchers will appreciate having a booklet to read. Web-based resources offer near-boundless flexibility in media, content and interactivity, but may also require extra support to create and edit.

How you present your stories also requires some thought. The inclusion of graphical presentation allows information to be conveyed far more effectively than text alone. Visual data also increases the accessibility and enhances the impact of the resource. The inclusion of timelines will allow complex and varied career information to be rationalised. Ensure you have the individual's permission to publish and reuse any information you include.

It is worth the extra time to include trialling a career story with some of the intended audience. This will allow you to refine your information collection and presentation to create a more useful final product.

Using the resource

Once complete, the final step is getting researchers to use the stories. Free-standing resources are useful for researchers to use in their own time, and have the potential to reach a wide audience. If your resource can also be used in career development workshops or by careers advisors in one-to-one career sessions, then impact will be greater. These materials could also prove valuable in annual appraisals or other career-orientated discussions. Whatever their potential, you need to ensure that people are aware of their existence and how to access them in order for these materials to reach their full potential.

The authors used career timelines to create Stories in Science: Postdoctoral Career Pathways, (www.postdoc-pathways.lifesci. dundee.ac.uk/) an interactive website and brochure that provide guidance for research staff seeking career progression.

Emma Compton-Daw and Nicola Phillips

Complementary ideas include **35** and **37**.

34 A tailored annual appraisal process for research staff

Our understanding of research staff experiences of the annual appraisal process at The University of Sheffield, UK, has been collated over a number of years through a variety of routes. These include research questionnaires, staff surveys, and by listening to the day-to-day conversations of our researchers and academics. There was not only unease and frustration about the process and its purpose in developing researcher careers, but also the principal investigators (PIs) line-managing researchers felt challenged to make the process a meaningful and useful exercise.

In addition, general guidance on appraisals needed adaptation to take into consideration the nature of research staff development within the modern higher education (HE) research funding landscape.

Drivers for change
We aimed to:

- acknowledge the range of contributions and achievements beyond research output;
- reinvigorate appraisal conversations to balance research focus with career development;
- reconcile conflicts of agenda between PI/project needs and research staff career development.

What did we do to achieve a change?
After two years of extensive consultation with research staff and academic groups we implemented changes across the institution. We designed:

- a tailored research staff appraisal form with subheadings 'Research', 'Teaching & Supervision', 'Administration', 'Continued Professional Development' and 'Career Aspirations';
- a supporting bank of coaching questions to enhance reflection and improve the quality of the conversations;
- guidance for departments on selection of appropriate reviewer(s) rather than defaulting to the PI every time.

The research-staff-endorsed recommendations were then approved at strategic level by faculty executive committees, human resources (HR), and the Joint Unions Committee (University and College Union and UNISON).

We met separately with representatives of each department to ensure departmental-level adoption, action planning, and communications plans. We ran workshops for research staff entitled 'Getting the most from your appraisal'.

How did the first year work in reality?
The process changes were adopted by all 16 departments and offered to all research staff – which in some departments not only covered research associates but also research assistants, fellows and academic staff. Reviewer changes were more challenging for departments to address, but in the first year three considered alternative approaches to having the PI as default reviewer.

Does it really make a difference?
We evaluated the year-one impact via an online PI/research staff survey (n=164) and in focus groups (n=17). 100 per cent of responding research staff (81) used the new form and, of those using the additional resources, 84 per cent found them useful. Only four per cent of respondents were not aware of the changes.

Research staff commented of the form: 'It focused the mind' and 'The clearly defined headings [are] really helpful to identify all the different aspects of my job and points to discuss.'

They also said the coaching questions 'really helped to facilitate the discussion with my PI around my career development rather than simply on my project.'

Additionally, the academic reviewers had a very positive experience with the changes, saying: 'questions on career pathway meant that this was considered by the reviewees beforehand as opposed to an afterthought as it had been in the past.' They also felt that 'the new form allowed the discussion during the meeting to be more meaningful' for the researcher.

Lessons learned
Making impactful changes took sustained effort, but the results are already proving very powerful to this staff group. The evaluation highlighted further improvements we will make to the process and the research staff appraisal form will continue, with step-by-step improvements and tweaks to find each department's best fit.

Lucy Lee and Sandrine Soubes

Complementary ideas include **37**.

35 Personal career benchmarking: helping researchers to set and achieve realistic career goals

The demands of higher education institutions on individual academic researchers are constantly changing. This is especially so in an increasingly international employment environment where institutional and organisational contexts may differ widely. Even within familiar environments, what brought success ten years ago may not do so now. As such, institutions, supervisors and principal investigators may not be effective at transmitting current knowledge downwards to early career staff, or they may transmit the wrong knowledge, or the knowledge they do transmit may be inappropriate for a researcher wanting to transfer to another environment. The tactics that worked for a research supervisor 15 years previously can be a highly influential source of guidance, however outdated.

So how can we help an early career researcher to plan their career development, and enjoy the benefits of opportunities worldwide, within such a changing, confusing and, at times, contradictory context?

Personal career benchmarking offers one alternative to being a hostage to fortune. It is a method of identifying, measuring and analysing best practices and standards among a given group of people in order to adopt those practices and achieve higher standards oneself. By doing so, researchers can gain clarity of understanding about performance levels required for gaining employment and promotion. Out of that they can develop and embark upon achieving realistic career goals with focus and efficiency, and with greater confidence in accomplishing a successful outcome. This process may initially require some facilitation, especially in the early stages, but the concepts of benchmarking could be woven into researcher development activities, facilitated sessions, or appraisal processes with relative ease – using a number of simple steps.

Current accomplishments

Ask your researchers to examine their current accomplishments. Who are they and what do they value most? What are they most proud of achieving and why? How long did it take to accomplish and with how much effort? This is an important first step, as an individual can view their own impressive academic accomplishments as less than stellar in an environment where everyone is very capable. Peer support or peer coaching can be a powerful ally here, since people often find it far easier to see strengths in others than in themselves.

Establish a rationale

Help your researchers to identify where they want to work, and why. Which country, which region or city, would they like to live and work within? It's good to set ambitious challenges, but realism is important. After all, there is only one richest person in the world. So researchers need to be careful which institutions or groups they target. An exploration of personal and professional values can help focus the rationale and subsequent targets.

Do your research

Encourage your researchers to actually research their target institutional environment. Which type of institution, which professional community, or discipline, which university or research institute, would they like to join?

Help focus their targets

Facilitate identification of what it takes to get a job in that environment and at that type of institution. What markers, or symbols, of achievement are necessary for gaining membership of that professional community? How many? At what level of quality? Are there any significant barriers to membership and success for them within that community?

Establish a 'fit'
By coaching, or facilitative questioning, help them to compare themselves, their values, and their accomplishments with what is necessary for membership of the target community. Are there any gaps and what is the nature of those gaps? Establish how hard they are prepared to work in closing those gaps. Point out that gaps in attributes and values are harder to close than quantity and quality of output gaps.

Specific reviewable goals
The next step is to encourage the setting of realistic and concrete goals, and then reviewing subsequent action over the following weeks and months. Individual one-to-one sessions, or peer support groups or action learning sets, can help reinforce this developmental process. The importance to researchers of networking within their target community should not be underestimated, though you may have to encourage them to make their achievements known.

Keep on going
Finally, success in any career path can often benefit from a good deal of luck. Failure and rejection are common, and so providing encouragement and fostering a resilient perspective may also be part of the researcher developer's role.

Peter Matanle

Complementary ideas include **33**, **37** and **39**.

36 Career impact through women-only programmes

Many universities are investigating or running 'women-only' researcher development activities as part of their commitment to positive action towards addressing gender inequality.

Reasoning

Within universities, women are still under-represented at the most senior levels. As such, junior and mid-career women in research often don't see themselves or their career aspirations reflected in senior teams. Individuals with both the ability and the aspiration to lead often find little access to encouragement, guidance or help as they negotiate a path alone through the academic status quo.

The Aurora programme run by The Leadership Foundation for Higher Education (LFHE) and the Springboard series of workshops offer multi-part career development programmes building cohorts of individuals across institutions (Aurora) and disciplines (Springboard). With demand for these programmes high, UK universities are offering complementary programmes developed in-house to reach a wider audience and create an environment where achieving gender equality is a priority.

The work of researcher developers focuses on relevant skill enhancement or career stage, addressing the similar priorities of the groups who attend. The intervention and activity are valued most by participants when aimed at those who have similar development and career-stage priorities (rather than just being gender specific). This is one of the key themes that comes through for participants from working with women-only groups.

The practicalities: a programme at The University of Edinburgh
Over the last five years the Institute for Academic Development

at The University of Edinburgh has made enterprise and strategic development programmes available to women-only cohorts. A particularly successful initiative is the Ingenious Women programme.

This residential programme (which has both non-residential and mixed-gender equivalents within the University's staff development offering) focuses on developing both research careers and research spin-out ideas with three 2-day workshops on the individual subjects of:

- 'Creativity – generating ideas and doing something with them';
- 'Cash – looking for ways to fund your ideas and take control of the money to develop them';
- 'Control – identifying ways to lead with your ideas and manage a balanced and purposeful life as you develop laterally or into a more senior leader'.

These three subjects are not unique to women, but delivery of this programme to an all-women audience helps to develop each theme with enough space to consider:

- how women challenge the status quo and create confident research and innovation role models for the future. This is achieved through small-group reflection, practice and action planning, leading to earlier application for promotion and innovation funding and development of spin-out social enterprises;
- the components of strategic thinking and actions through presentation, role-model speakers and reading. These provide resources for these leaders to bring to their teams and collaborations to achieve more on behalf of their research groups, institutions and areas of expertise;
- the role of engaging and effective networks for career development and enhancing current practice. This aspect is central to Ingenious Women, which offers multiple opportunities to work with every single member of the cohort

in one-to-one and group settings over a nine-week period where the residential elements are central but not crucial to the programme. This reduces the sense of isolation for those women in departments when there are few, if any, female leaders and sometimes a woefully small number of female peers. In the case of each cohort these supportive and peer mentoring relationships have continued significantly beyond the facilitated part of the programme;

• how, since recruiting boards at all levels tend to hire in their own image, all researchers need to be equipped with both the skills and confidence to communicate their expertise and experience to recruiting audiences. Peer discussion, invited guest speakers, reading and action planning to find mentors and role models beyond the programme enable participants to prepare to face panels with a greater range of strategic language, evidence of political understanding, and influencing skills, thus leading to more applications submitted for promotion, secondment or funding by the participants in these cohorts.

But what of having children? Maternity leave? Balancing work and home with part-time work? Yes, women-only development programmes cover these things. However, they should not be *about* these things. They are about equipping women with the knowledge, skills and perspectives to take responsibility for their own leadership development, engaging with both male and female colleagues around them constructively, confidently and capably towards a future where academia enjoys a 50:50 gender balance at all levels of leadership.

Sara Shinton, Nicola Cuthbert and Janet Wilkinson

Complementary ideas include **27**, **37**, **38** and **39**.

37 Developing aspiring fellows – more than luck!

Fellowship Ahoy! was a research project that investigated the experiences of researchers who have gained a fellowship award. Successful fellows often describe themselves in modest terms as 'just lucky', or as being in the right place at the right time, and this project asked the question 'What got you to the right place at the right time?'

Researchers who aspire to research fellowships cite numerous barriers to applying for awards, and again the notion of luck arises. A major component of this is the idea that a researcher needs to be 'lucky enough' to have a supportive principal investigator (PI) who will give the permissions, time and space to apply, and afford them the opportunities to practise and develop an independent profile. Further barriers reported include 'not having good ideas', 'not having time', and 'not being independent yet'. A key purpose in investigating fellows' experiences was to highlight the varied accounts of how researchers move towards and beyond their applications. The project aimed to demonstrate the diverse backgrounds, routes in, career paths, and circumstances of successful independent researchers. It further aimed to characterise in detail what is actively done by researchers in the preparation and application for a fellowship award.

What the research involved

A multi-institution (eight research-intensive HEIs) research study, funded by the LFHE Small Development Project scheme, used interviews to collect the stories of 25 fellows (13 female, 12 male; 17 UK, 8 non-UK; 18 STEM, 7 non-STEM) on how they made it happen, and which colleagues' support they felt had been essential to their success. The project was more than academic research, and a key aim for the study was to develop learning resources and recommendations from the data, to support the thinking, planning and development of researchers.

What the fellows said

The accounts of what fellows did, how, and who helped them, show that independent researchers are hugely active in their own development. Key areas they seek to develop are: awareness of funding opportunities; application and interview techniques; self-confidence; original project ideas; and resilience following unsuccessful applications.

Fellows achieved this intense development via the input, critique, endorsement and support of others. A key self-development activity was joining research networks, seeking out new contacts, and activating those contacts for different supporting roles, such as shaping ideas, critiquing draft applications, project collaboration, and in helping the applicant to navigate the complex internal and external systems and processes of research funding.

This work demonstrates that in addition to the recognised element of luck in gaining research funding, success in gaining fellowship awards is enabled by the agency of early career researchers, acted through professional networks.

How can we help?

Initiatives that support researchers to develop within the context of their networks can support this further. In particular:

- making visible the varied routes, contexts, struggles and prior experiences that can lead to achieving a fellowship award;
- facilitating access to independent career support via cross-institution mentoring programmes;
- a meaningful appraisal and reward process for early career researchers that recognises their contributions and supports tailored career reflection;
- broadening networks beyond the institution by encouraging joint or reciprocal events, e.g. invited speaker series;

- supporting cohorts of researchers to identify small external funding awards, and navigate the whole process of gaining, managing, and delivering on research funding;
- helping researchers demonstrate, and PIs recognise, the mutual benefits of developing a new independent research leader.

Two free online learning resources have been produced that combine learning from the literature, tools, tips and techniques, with real data from the study: www.sheffield.ac.uk/ris/ecr/ mentoring/connected; www.sheffield.ac.uk/ris/ecr/mentoring/ inspired.

Kay Guccione

Complementary ideas include **33**, **34**, **36** and **38**.

38 Designing groups for fellowship applications and grant writing

As researchers develop towards independence, it is vital they take control of their career and shift their emphasis from delivering projects to focusing on generating ideas, writing funding proposals and identifying their own research agenda. The University of Sheffield, UK, established groups to aid researchers through this challenging transition.

These groups facilitate information sharing about the funding landscape, build understanding of the 'art' of writing proposals, and provide a supportive community. The programme is delivered in partnership with established academics and fellows, which anchors the context in the lived experiences of successfully funded researchers, but also ensures that researchers raise their awareness of institutional professional staff support and processes.

Group composition

The group size varies (5–25 participants) and each cohort includes heterogeneity of aspirations, ambitions and career stages. Groups mix people unsure of the steps to achieve their future career with those building towards independent academic careers, and some already in the process of writing research funding proposals.

Structured to support action

On recruitment, each participant commits to attend and engage with six 2-hour facilitated monthly meetings. This timescale is designed to create momentum for action, help set milestones, and stimulate the embedding of new habits: regular ideas development; writing; research funding awareness; and horizon scanning.

Ground rules (e.g. confidentiality) are agreed so that new research ideas and draft proposals can be shared. Each researcher is encouraged to set personal goals.

Subsequent meetings focus on particular elements of a research career: publication strategies; developing a research niche; initiating independent collaboration as principal investigator; small grant applications; the perspective of grant reviewers; interview technique. Successful applications are shared and discussed, and fellows share their stories, encouraging questions and discussion.

At the end of each session, action points were shared. At subsequent meetings, participants report back on actions taken, ideas and information gained, or challenges faced. This monthly check-in enables small steps and encourages the group to learn from each other. This sharing, in combination with the experiences from contributing academics allows myths to be dispelled, illuminates invisible academic practices, and helps researchers realise that they are not alone in lacking confidence, that resilience and pro-activity are key, that an ongoing process of idea development is crucial, and that not simply waiting 'to be ready' is paramount to transition.

Managing groups effectively

Due to the heterogeneity of the group and differing workload pressures there may be irregular participant numbers, so the facilitator needs flexibility and an adaptable programme plan. There are no expectations of specific outcomes (such as 'after six months you must have a written fellowship or funding application') as some researchers are only exploring options and gathering information.

To reinforce group cohesion and provide support to achieve action points, we encourage participants to 'buddy' in pairs and meet in between each workshop. No monitoring of buddy meetings takes place.

One area that the group emphasise and support is the need to find ways of working in a complementary and open manner with principal investigators in order to negotiate research boundaries and ownership of future research ideas as researchers progress towards independent research projects.

Value added and evaluation
Researchers join the peer support group with different aims and so complete the programme with different outcomes. We found it helpful to measure programme impact as an individual's progression towards their own goals set at the onset. Short-term evaluation data show an increase in: knowledge and awareness of funding processes; writing skills; developing self-awareness of career intentions; and making applications to small funding sources. We will need to examine the programme's influence in facilitating longer-term transitions.

Sandrine Soubes

Complementary ideas include **35, 36, 37, 40** and **41**.

39 Progression pathways – supporting researchers with promotions

Supporting researchers to make the transition to lectureships can be one of the most challenging tasks for researcher developers. Overall, in the UK, many institutions show a strong commitment to recruiting, nurturing and promoting researchers. However, the processes involved are not always transparent. In institutions where defined reward and recognition processes do exist, we have found awareness amongst researchers and their managers to be low. How aware are you of such processes within your institution? How do you support researchers aspiring to lectureships in other institutions?

Commitment

The University of Manchester has a long-standing commitment to reward and promote all staff, underpinned with a financial model that factors promotion when budget setting. Researchers and academic staff are invited to apply for promotion against clear criteria and guidance on progression from researcher through to professor. We have three distinct promotion pathways with parity between them: promotion on the grounds of research; teaching and learning; or both. These criteria explicitly document the evidence required for each grade or position on a university-wide promotion timeline.

Policy to practice

As researcher developers we play a crucial role in raising awareness of career development and promotion policies and processes amongst researchers and PIs. We support and enable researchers to build evidence, take stock of achievements and gaps, and action plan for development. We have developed a suite of training and support materials around promotion:

- Booklets of successful applications across levels;
- Videos from promotion panel members and senior research leaders giving insider knowledge and helping to clarify promotion criteria;
- Workshops aligned to the promotion timetable delivered in partnership with 'promotion champions'.

Champions are senior academics appointed within each area or discipline to act as mentors. Workshops are underpinned by one-to-one coaching sessions and CV clinics with researcher developers.

Empowering researchers

Through this development suite we empower researchers to apply for promotion. We have seen a year-on-year increase in researchers applying, and 77 per cent of applicants succeeded recently. Through this process, researcher visibility and research impact have been strengthened, resulting in researcher representation on promotion panels and senior leadership teams. Researcher promotions are celebrated through a Dean's reception and email announcements.

Working in partnership with senior management, HR and researchers

As researcher developers we gained first-hand experience of the promotion process, through sitting on promotions panels. This enabled us to articulate the importance of a rounded CV, documenting and evidencing across all promotion criteria. We report to institutional committees (e.g. Equality and Diversity and HR) and, by working with HR, we have ensured balanced and transparent promotion panel membership and the use of inclusive and specific researcher language in documentation.

Development approaches

An experiential approach to promotions workshops has created an environment where researchers can openly discuss their development needs. Researchers benefit from interdisciplinary discussions which dispel local myths and perceived barriers to promotion. Coaching has been a powerful tool that has built confidence and self-belief, so researchers no longer feel they must wait to be invited to apply for promotion. Crucially, all researcher developers at the university have been supported in gaining coaching qualifications.

Moving forward

We aim to further increase the number of researchers being promoted. To sustain this, grant and fellowship applicants need to routinely cover the annual increments incurred as salary progression or financial reward in all applications. Working in partnership with PIs and researchers, we aim to create a culture where promotions are discussed more regularly. PI engagement is critical and we will work to further develop PI mentoring and coaching skills to enable effective career conversations.

Judith Williams and Rachel Cowen

Complementary ideas include **34**, **35**, **36** and **40**.

Progression pathways **39**

Chapter 8
Programmes for special purposes

40 Developing interdisciplinary researcher communities: the Crucible programme

Collaboration and interdisciplinarity are key concerns of modern research culture. However, early career researchers may lack experience or opportunities to break out of their disciplinary comfort zone. Further challenges in early career transition include departmental isolation, limited experience of non-academic partners, difficulties in accessing funding to explore preliminary and risky ideas, and dilemmas in framing research interests in the context of funding schemes.

The Sheffield Crucible, an adaptation of the UK's national NESTA Crucible (crucibleinabox.nesta.org.uk) recruits researchers from a single institution and aims to broaden research horizons towards making interdisciplinarity a default position. Crucible provides space and time to explore new forms of collaboration.

Programme ethos and structure
Participants are selected to create a cohort that is diverse in terms of disciplinary perspective, career level, gender and cultural background, but with a commitment to the idea of collaborative research.

The Crucible participants (30 per programme) meet during three two-day residential workshops (called 'labs') over the course of six months. The residential element (in a venue providing comfort, inspiration and conviviality) is, we believe, critical in developing a sense of community, and nurturing truthful and trusting relationships. Crucible needs a programme manager who really believes in the power of collaborative interactions and fully engages in building this new community.

Each residential 'lab' has a particular focus:

- Lab 1 – external engagement (e.g. media, public, policy);
- Lab 2 – the challenge of fostering creativity and innovation within collaborations;
- Lab 3 – reflecting on individual skills to work in interdisciplinary teams.

Contributors include senior academics with extensive experience of diverse interdisciplinary projects, and external professionals as sources of inspiration (e.g. artists, storytellers, policy makers, journalists).

Experiencing interdisciplinary collaborations

To move from thinking about interdisciplinary collaborations towards experiencing them, participants are given three months (following the final Lab) to write a funding application, thus enabling potential collaborations to mature and ideas to evolve. The University offers Crucible seed-funding for up to 11 months for project proposals of £5,000–£10,000. Projects have to include participants from different disciplines (sometimes these are external partners). Proposals have tended to include three researchers, though we have received proposals with up to nine collaborators.

Seed-funding applicants pitch the potential projects to the public during a local science festival, and we ask the public to vote on which project they would want us to fund. Ultimately a cross-faculty committee decides on the funding, though the public vote is incorporated into the process. 18 projects have been funded from 38 applications across two programmes.

The funding selection committee needs to understand interdisciplinary approaches, and grasp the purpose of Crucible and the seed-funding (that is, explorative and unusual projects).

Evidencing the value

After the projects have concluded, it is useful to run a short fourth lab to allow participants to reflect and consider their next steps. Success for Crucible is about the experiential learning of the collaborative process and not the specific outcomes of the projects themselves. Crucible is a considerable undertaking of time and effort on the part of the researchers, but participants have reported very positive impacts. These collaborative experiences have contributed towards:

- successful fellowship and lectureship applications;
- novel curriculum development;
- new research project co-supervision;
- enhanced integration of researchers within the University.

Moreover, Crucible at Sheffield has directly led to patent applications, art exhibitions, resources for patient groups, larger external funding bids, public engagement opportunities, social enterprise collaborations and media work, and also – but not least – a number of research publications.

Ultimately, Crucible brings great personal rewards in seeing the emergence of fascinating projects, in observing the budding of long-lasting interactions, and in building strong relationships between research leaders of the future.

Sandrine Soubes

Complementary ideas include **38** and **41**.

41 Multi-disciplinary sandpits for researcher development

Sandpits (sometimes called sandboxes or ideas labs), are a means of exploring ideas or addressing research problems with the aim of developing multi-disciplinary research proposals. Sandpits are often used by the UK research councils to promote multidisciplinary and collaborative working practices, but they can be applied to a wide range of contexts. They can be run over a day or for as long as five days. A typical sandpit might include presentations, videos, discussions, workshops, and 'speed dating' and will bring together a broad range of participants – academics (from PhD student to professor) and external partners (business, government, funders, communities of interest or members of the public) – all relevant to, and with interest in the area being discussed.

Optional element: speed dating

Speed dating can be used as a fantastic ice breaker and energiser. Participants sit side by side in two rows of chairs facing each other. They have two minutes (a minute each) to discuss an area of interest, problem, solution, etc. with the person opposite them before a bell rings and one side moves along one seat. It is best to hold speed dating early in the event so that people get to know each other and make connections that will be strengthened through conversation throughout the sandpit.

Although sandpits are commonly used as a means of collaboration and exploration, researchers in some disciplines traditionally work in silos and it can be difficult to engage them in this way. They may not see the benefit of such an approach, they may feel they have no time to contribute to it, or they may perceive sharing their research ideas as a threat.

However, there are many benefits for participants. These include: developing networking and presentation skills; confidence building; sharing good practice; problem solving; and exploring their research ideas with others. There are also potential benefits for external organisations, including new collaborations and research partners, and for the institution, such as: research funding; PhD studentships; transformative research; secondments to and from industry and other external organisations; establishment of new research centres; and job creation.

Pointers for an effective sandpit

It is important to employ the right facilitator. This could be a professional facilitator, an academic, or a researcher developer. The key roles of a facilitator are to present the topic and to encourage the participants to discuss the 'big issues', explore how they can contribute to addressing them, and create plans to resolve them. The facilitator will need to be able to effectively engage all the participants and keep them focused. They need to be supportive and trustworthy and be removed enough from the research that the participants don't feel their ideas are threatened. A good facilitator will plan well for contingencies and use a wide range of strategies to engage the participants and draw out information.

For breakout sessions, a smaller space with round tables works best as this encourages more people to participate and ask questions. (Try to get those who need presentation experience or confidence to feed back their small-group discussion to the larger group, and give them plenty of encouragement.)

Sandpits as a means of support for researcher development can bring about great changes for a small contribution. The outcomes for participants can include new skills, collaborations, promotions and funding.

Rhian Melita Morris

Complementary ideas include **32**, **38** and **40**.

42 New models, new opportunities: supporting larger-scale doctoral training programmes

In the UK, the last decade has seen the emergence of new models of formal cohort-based doctoral training (such as Doctoral Training Centres), which place development centre-stage. 'Training' in this context refers to the whole learning and development experience of the early career researcher. Researchers attend workshops and groups, complete career plans, engage in non-academic work experience, and develop strong communities – and so graduate ready to have impact in a range of roles and sectors.

These insights are offered to help you understand the key features of formal doctoral cohort models and the demands they place on academics, researchers and researcher developers.

Co-creation
If you invest in understanding the purpose of these cohort learning models and the value you can add to their design and delivery, these are great opportunities for you as researcher developers to innovate and to demonstrate your expertise. Build relationships with your research support office so they can connect you directly with academics preparing funding proposals. Familiarise yourself with application forms so you can prepare core text that can be provided quickly at short notice, or tailored if you're invited to contribute. Meet the principal investigators to discuss the training the doctoral researchers will receive and how you can complement this. Once recruited, doctoral students will drive the evolution of your provision, so be ready to include their emerging ideas in future planning.

Co-delivery and collaboration
Another characteristic of cohort models is the collaboration between disciplines and institutions. It's not uncommon for researchers to move between institutions for meetings, secondments, or training,

so benefiting from the facilities and expertise at all partner locations. This will include your work, so you need develop processes and arrangements for opening up your courses to students from other institutions. This may be a simple reciprocal agreement or one that involves a financial exchange. If you are asked to develop events or workshops that are tailored for the cohort, does this fall under your normal work remit, or will the extra work need to attract funding? It's worth defining the service packages you can offer, and agreeing the scope of each.

'Two-tier' issues
Cohorts are the preferred doctoral training model for some funders, but departments will often also have students who are not in the cohort. Researcher developers need to be wary of the emergence of a two-tier system that delivers very different student experiences to the two groups. Can you arrange things so you open up some of the enhanced support and opportunities to students outside these cohorts too? How can you be inclusive and offer equitable doctoral packages?

Evaluation and monitoring
The high level of resource and staffing investment in these models brings more scrutiny to the doctoral experience. Proposals and reports need to include evidence of the uptake, and also the outcomes and impact of development activities. Evaluation must be robust and may involve expanding your current approaches to feedback. Can you involve a local specialist in survey design, or service evaluation? How does your data evidence that the aims of the funder are being achieved?

Doctoral training cohort models have researchers at their heart and provide researcher developers with great opportunities to innovate and collaborate, provided they invest time in understanding these models and building relationships with the users and with the academics and funders involved.

Sara Shinton

Complementary ideas include **15** and **51**.

New models, new opportunities **42**

Chapter 9
Extending your reach

43 Research staff associations: a key development ally

What are research staff associations?
Research staff associations (RSAs), are groups of research staff within a department, institution or even geographical region. An RSA may be initiated by an institution or by the research staff themselves and usually fulfils two roles: to provide a voice for this staff group and a sense of community for its members. In addition, and increasingly, RSAs take on researcher career development responsibilities.

The activities RSAs undertake can be many and varied: organising seminars, workshops and social events; assessing and awarding funding for career development activities or projects; raising the profile and visibility of research staff in policy and contractual decisions; representing their staff group, and their needs, on institutional committees.

Why should an RSA be an essential part of any researcher development provision?
RSAs provide experiential development opportunities beyond day-to-day research: fulfilling leadership roles; managing large-scale projects; and influencing policy. Previous members of RSAs quote these experiences as key in their progression to the next stage of both academic and non-academic careers.

Mutual benefit
Significant insight into researcher development needs can be gained via RSAs, and these engaged individuals can help design and improve programmes of learning. RSAs can be a test bed for new initiatives, offering feedback from the user perspective, and helping to promote the finished products.

Researcher developers play an essential role in RSA success too, by offering practical and logistical support to members and activities, embedding the group within an institution, and bridging the gap between junior and senior voices.

Key challenges for researcher developers lie in setting up an RSA, and in maintaining continuity and sustainability in the long term. Some common issues and suggestions for how a researcher developer can help overcome these are detailed here.

Getting started
- *Gaining a critical mass* – find and encourage 'first followers'; consider word-of-mouth avenues to nurture enthusiasm rather than blanket campaigns;
- *Clarity and purpose* – facilitate remit setting for the RSA: what are is its vision, aims and terms of reference?
- *Securing funding* – identify and provide support during any application process to communicate the value of the RSA and what it will deliver;
- *Connecting research staff to decision-making processes* – provide guidance and reassurance in influencing institutional direction.

Assuring sustainability
- *Accountability and responsibility* – ensure the RSA is trusted and accountable at an institutional level. To whom do they report their progress?
- *Replenish numbers* – continue to find and encourage new members; help secure their access to web resources and printed materials;
- *Momentum* – provide guidance on effective committee structures and procedures, and project management tools. Support efficient committee handovers;
- *Profile and visibility* – help secure access to web and printed materials; champion your RSA within the institution; invite them to events and meetings; and share your networks.

RSAs play an important role in a researcher-led cluster of development opportunities; we should be nurturing their input at every opportunity to ensure our work is relevant and engaging.

Emma Compton-Daw

Complementary ideas include **2**, **3**, **7**, **31** and **48**.

44 The pedagogy of supervision in a new supervisor programme

Why do we need this?
From discussions with research students, we all know that their supervisory teams are at the centre of their worlds: what supervisors say is taken by students as the 'gospel truth' and what supervisors do will undoubtedly 'make or break' the research degree experience for their students. So, positively influence the approaches of supervisors and we improve the learning journey for generations of research students.

How do we do this?
We don't need supervisors with superhuman powers, just ones that use supervisory pedagogies (reasoned teaching approaches) wisely. We want them to focus on goals to meet their and their students' learning aspirations. We want them to make sense of their situations to make well informed supervisory choices. We want them to make good use of supervisory meetings and assessment processes to give students good learning experiences. And we can use new supervisor programmes explicitly to explore decision making to build a bank of supervisory approaches for a range of situations and students.

What key points do we need to remember?
These are really obvious when someone else says it! But 'keep it real' so supervisors engage in a meaningful way, 'know common narratives' so we can facilitate discussions effectively, and 'be careful with semantics' so we don't alienate ourselves or the audience.

Keep it real
Let's make it real and therefore invaluable by helping supervisors build authentic supervisory pedagogies. We can use discussions

to explore their values and beliefs about the research degree to uncover their desires for student learning and supervision. These desires translate into valued goals.

Know common narratives
Absolutely all supervisors value learning that 1. develops their students' ability to do research, 2. offers benefits to society, and 3. uses research because it discovers new things. So, use this information like gold dust: we can sprinkle these ideas into conversations to ignite practice-sharing discussions and also use them to group personal goals into three themes when drawing ideas together.

Be careful with semantics
Use the 'm' (manager) and 'p' (process) words sparingly! Above all else we need to remember that inexperienced supervisors are 'allergic' to discussions that frame them as a 'manager' and emphasise 'processes' over research practices. They don't fit with the ideal that supervisors should 'be the expert', 'work autonomously' and not be 'diverted from research towards form-filling exercises' – I'm sure you're already thinking that there is a discussion required in these areas as a priority, and you're right!

And we can also balance manager-related discussions with discussions on other role types and highlight the benefits of using processes strategically, tactically and operationally. You'll never remove the hoop-jumping feeling that supervisors have about completing processes, but at least they will see the point and use them effectively.

What results can we expect?
I've described how we can help supervisors align supervisory approaches with desirable learning outcomes to plant ideas as seeds for developing supervisory pedagogies for reflective practitioners. Although this is of huge benefit for both supervisors and their students, it takes time for desired results to be seen in practice. But there are some quick wins for our supervisors which

you will see immediately. Here, we introduce supervisors to a new language of supervision so they can explicitly analyse their context and decision-making processes. And even by the end of the discussions you will see signs that they feel more comfortable and confident with the approaches they discuss using in the future.

Mark Proctor

Complementary ideas include **16** and **19**.

45 Livecasting

Sharing what is happening, live, in classrooms and offices is now both easy and cheap. The options for sharing live content range from Twitter updates, to what is essentially a TV station running through a handheld tablet. Livecasting technologies hold enormous potential for broadening the reach of researcher development activities and giving more people access to content and learning opportunities. However, the idea of being 'live' and visible to an audience you can't see can be a cause of great anxiety for many people.

Choosing your tools

The nature of your event will determine the sort of tools you will need. The key considerations are how the event is staged, audience participation model, cost, and desired quality of the livecast. If an event is staged as a conventional single performance piece where quality is important, for example a lecture or a Three Minute Thesis final (threeminutethesis.org/), consider hiring professionals who can manage the process for you. It's best to use local providers where possible, as they may know your venue; try Googling 'livestream professionals' and your district or area name. A word of caution: professionals should not be brought in at the last minute! Careful planning is crucial. You don't want to find out just before your event goes live that their equipment obscures the view of your live audience members.

At the other end of the quality spectrum, at a casual seminar in a small room it might be sufficient to use a tablet running a live broadcasting app. These apps create a link that can be shared on a range of social media sites and let you bring in an instant, worldwide audience. You can improve quality significantly by simply mounting the tablet on a stand. In between these extremes is the webinar, which is usually broadcast without a live audience physically present through specialist learning management platforms. Webinars are similar to radio broadcasts and can be quite draining for the presenter.

Researcher developers as performers

Many researcher developers are reluctant to be photographed, let alone broadcast live on the web. These fears range from the mundane – the clothes they are wearing or how fat they might appear on camera – to more serious concerns about performance and content being discoverable on the web. These fears relate to being judged as lacking in some way by unspecified others. These fears are usually unjustified, but it doesn't mean they are not real. It is never a good idea to push yourself or others too far out of personal comfort zones. The researchers you work with are likely to have similar doubts and insecurities as you do. Briefing people carefully on who is watching and where the footage will be made available is important.

Becoming comfortable and proficient at livecasting involves an investment of time and effort, but the power to literally bring people into the room makes it a powerful tool for building communities.

Inger Mewburn

Complementary ideas include **3** and **46**.

46 Taking a development programme abroad

As universities expand in a global environment the need to extend researcher development from a central campus to international satellite campuses or to other researchers based abroad presents a significant challenge. In some situations there may be local experts to provide support, but in others there may not. While the issues presented are numerous, and can be specific to individual situations, some common elements underpin success in these endeavours.

Understand the culture
Understanding the culture is very important. The international campus culture will be heavily influenced by the local wider culture, as well as the educational backgrounds of the academics and researchers. Many elements will influence the overall culture, including dominant funders, dominant disciplines, where the researchers have worked and studied in the past, teaching–research balance of roles, and so on. Whatever the situation, an international campus is likely to be a very different environment from the main home campus. Understanding how the campus works is the first step towards success.

Understand the context
If possible, visit the international site and learn about how the researchers work there, gain a good understanding of the local and regional research environment. Identify what local networks exist to support researchers, how the funding works, what conferences exist, and what impact and public engagement opportunities there are. Gain a good understanding of the management approaches, the challenges faced and the local priorities. Ensure you have a good understanding of the local resources such as rooms, IT support, etc. All of these are likely to be very different from those present at the home campus.

Get connected locally

Build good relationships with local 'gatekeepers', local researchers and any staff who may be willing to support development activities. Who are the local experts you will call on to help develop researchers locally? Also build a good network of local contacts to keep you informed of local affairs and changes.

Identify what to focus on

It is unlikely you will be able to replicate a full programme, so you will need to identify the key development priorities, which will, no doubt, be contested by some stakeholders. Identify:

1) what will make the biggest difference;
2) what will be supported by the local senior management;
3) what will engage the researchers.

Focus on where these overlap.

Delivery options

Consider carefully the possible approaches to delivery. Face-to-face in person will probably be the most popular with both developers and researchers but may be restricted to short intensive periods during visits. Remote face-to-face via Skype or other video tools is also an option, but this will need specific resources from both sites as well as technical support at both sites. Access to appropriate rooms may be difficult and consideration of different time zones and learning cultures is important. Fully online development provision (synchronous or asynchronous) can be effective, but needs significant preparation and appropriate skills, both in design as well as moderation. Engagement of researchers who are unused to online learning may prove difficult and high dropout rates or long completion times are common. Whatever approach is used, having good web-based resources to supplement the other development activities is important, as is providing good signposting to external sources of development support (such as funders' web pages, open resources, specific TED talks, etc.)

Balance between group and individual support

All researchers benefit from individual support, but getting the right balance between group activities and individual support is difficult. Coaching and mentoring can both provide good, focused support for individuals and can cover areas that broader group approaches may not cover. Encouraging and enabling strong peer support can also be beneficial.

Evaluate

As with all development, you need to understand what is working well, what is not working and what your next steps should be. As the target audience, as well as the local environment, will be different at different sites, one cannot assume that a successful approach at the main campus will have a similar level of success at an international campus. Be sure to plan appropriate evaluation into all new activities to inform changes and improvements to your approaches.

Rob Daley

Complementary ideas include **2** and **7**.

Chapter 10
Embedding value and developing a researcher developer career

47 Researcher developers exist without the job title

Someone with the title of researcher developer or remit to develop researchers will likely have a very clear sense of identity and responsibility to do just that. Standard practice has been that this is done by taking researchers out of their day-to-day environments to engage in development, only to return them when the 'development' has happened.

The success of learning can be seen in a change in behaviour or practice, so the developer is likely to see the impact greatly increased if they have considered the environment the researcher is returning to. Metaphorically, if the developer waters the flower and sees it blossom in the immediacy of the interaction, that flower may well wither and die if returned to an arid or scorching environment.

Many staff at our institutions have a role to play in researcher development. None is more overlooked than the role of the academic as researcher developer. The academic, whether as supervisor of doctoral researchers or manager of research staff, is potentially the most influential 'developer' in that individual's sphere. This is closely followed by the day-to-day culture in which that researcher is employed.

There is a need to create an informal yet extensive team of developers, connected by a shared desire to support researchers. A team does not exist because a structure chart is put on a website, but has reality from the behaviours and interactions of those within it.

Teams of developers can be both fluid and static. Creating initiatives where academics are integral or even essential is an excellent opportunity for widening the team of researcher developers and embedding the value of learning and development across the organisation. From a programme or event point of view, this is most commonly seen in mentoring schemes or having academics contribute to activities as expert panel members or speakers at induction events.

More significantly though, researcher development by academics is achieved through the utilisation of university-wide strategies such as annual appraisal. The appraisal is a process where expectations can be set and cultures reinforced, such as the value of researchers engaging in development planning and conversing with their managers. Managers can receive clear guidance on the value these conversations have and the methods to make them productive.

To enable real change to occur, the formal researcher developer needs to be mindful of their responsibility to be a leader of change in order to create and maintain a culture of development across the institution. They should have the drive and opportunity to shape policies and practices (such as for appraisal), offering support to managers along the way.

In summary, a collaborative approach to researcher development is essential to success. A variety of staff inputting to reach a common goal – that of 'developed' and productive researchers – will undoubtedly lead to a flexible and evolving researcher development culture. Academics must be viewed as a resource and as an integral part of any institution's researcher development offer.

Bryony Portsmouth

Complementary ideas include **1**, **10**, **18**, **19**, **26**, **27** and **34**.

48 Tuning in to research staff: recommendations to PIs

Principal investigators (PIs) invent, create and disseminate excellent research that, in many cases, could not happen without the input of research staff, who bring intellectual commitment, creativity and a thirst for knowledge. By encouraging and enabling PIs to tune in to the value, experiences and needs of research staff, researcher developers can ensure that researchers are at their best and most motivated.

It's essential to understand what the experiences and needs of research staff actually are. Three workshops run by researchers, for researchers, at The University of Sheffield, UK, sought to elicit this, through story-telling exercises, and by carving out time and space for reflection. Participants of the workshops shared their experiences of being researchers and discussions were distilled into a collection of recommendations to PIs on getting the best from researchers. Five suggestions are highlighted here and could be incorporated into supervisor development.

1. The curious case of the invisible researcher
Research staff are at their best when they are 'visible' – invited to meetings, introduced to colleagues and fully integrated. By encouraging departments to adopt induction activities for new staff, researcher developers can help to broaden connections beyond the narrow confines of a research project.

2. Time for professional development
The Concordat to Support the Career Development of Researchers encourages research staff to spend time each month on development activities as part of their work. Researcher developers play an important role in familiarising researchers and PIs with this policy document.

3. Progression, promotion and retention

Many researchers want to pursue a career in research itself, and not just as a stepping stone to a lectureship. Researcher developers can encourage PIs to talk to researchers about their intended career path, and could influence mechanisms and processes for the progression, promotion and retention of talented research staff.

4. Working together

PIs need to think about how they can work in partnership with their researchers, especially in publishing together and applying for funding. Researcher developers are the link between PIs, their researchers and the university's research income managers and can broker discussions of future funding possibilities.

5. Location, location, location

All too often PIs have not ensured that researchers have a permanent workspace in a location that allows them to network with other researchers and members of academic staff. Researcher developers can help to remind PIs of the need for a permanent workspace, and encourage dedicated working areas for researchers.

These messages can be effectively delivered to PIs by combining a number of approaches. These could include electronic mailshots or paper postcards as well as more formal methods, such as a workshop for PIs, vision statements and policy documents.

Tuning in to research staff can be very beneficial for PIs too. By supporting PIs to act on the kinds of issues identified above, researcher development professionals can help to ensure that research projects are delivered on time, outputs (including publications) are maximised and staff skill levels are at their best.

At a time when concerns are being raised that fixed-term researchers have become invisible within their faculties, and even within academia as a whole, it's crucial that researcher developers, PIs and other HE leaders tune in to the value of research staff. They hold an important, but in many ways unique, position within academia and the experiences and needs of research staff can vary greatly from one individual to the next.

By supporting research staff to share experiences, and by helping PIs to act on this information, researcher development professionals can play a key role in maximising the potential of their researchers.

Richard Ward

Complementary ideas include **2**, **34** and **49**.

49 Development scepticism – reason and reaction

I once led a research fellowship induction and a senior university leader was asked to give the welcome address to this prestigious group. Now, I'm paraphrasing a little here, but his speech, in essence, was: 'I never did this sort of training and it never harmed me'.

This kind of killed the developmental vibe.

Recent years have seen huge changes in the development environment; but most pronounced is the simple increase in expectation that researchers will have access to formalised development. However, in certain quarters, there still remains considerable scepticism of, and resistance towards, 'developmental' activity. This scepticism may come from researchers themselves, academic supervisors and seniors, or even from institutional management. More likely it results from a combination of these protagonists.

Any sort of intervention (workshop, action-learning, mentoring) will appeal to different individuals differently, but overall scepticism can mean wholesale resistance to the concept of any external 'support'.

So why, given all our efforts, do we face scepticism, and what can be done?

Look to ourselves
Principally, we must look to ourselves. Doubt about our academic place, uncertainty about our value and an over-eagerness to please all undermine our credibility. Ours is a new discipline; it is still evolving and learning what works. As a community we must remember that some practice, as we have evolved, was not as

good as we would now want it to be. This legacy remains today inside anyone who had to attend a compulsory lecture-based thesis-writing course *after* they'd written-up... It is important to acknowledge this heritage immediately with sceptics. After all, pretending that everything is and always has been fantastic is ethically and academically dubious.

Evidence value not activity

Ask yourself, what value does development add, and can you provide evidence that a journal reviewer would accept? Are there baseline competency data? Can you show clear progression post intervention? Are your data triangulated with feedback from (for instance) a participant's supervisor? If the answer to these questions is 'no', then that's potentially why our efforts are resisted. We are keen to list activities, but unless we provide rigorous, longitudinal and not simply perception-based evidence that developed researchers become better researchers then we are on academically questionable ground. After all, our sceptics look for weak arguments in every journal article they consume.

Institutional culture and role models

What institutionally has traditionally been rewarded in research: development-focused people leadership, or high paper output and a mince-grinder of researchers from which some rise? If it's the latter (and it often is) then development is fighting a rearguard action from the start. Moreover, if I wanted to 'sell' researcher development to individuals I would market to female, international and mature students. These (not exclusively, obviously) are groups thirsty for development opportunities. Yet look at the core demographic of academic supervisors. It's only my opinion, but I see a mismatch.

If academic supervisors a) aren't keen adopters of researcher development and b) have been successful then their scepticism will endure. Our landscape, fortunately, is now changing; our industry has become more 'professionalised' and needs professionals to work in it. So, it is worth helping sceptics to realise that they may not have done 'courses' but they did develop. They just spent large amounts of their own time and energy figuring things out in isolation.

Champions and sounding boards
Developers have long known the value of champions to help spread a message; so it is worth seeking out supportive role models, earning their trust (rigorous evidence helps) and asking them to advocate on your behalf.

If what we do is well received, encourage all stakeholders to share their experience (testimonials, social media). Our participants and delegates must be our strongest champions, because you can guarantee that if their experience is not good they will certainly be vocal.

One of the worst mistakes we can make is to bypass sceptics, who can make excellent sounding boards for new ideas and can help us to strengthen our programmes and marketing. Moreover, researcher development needs to explain what it is not. Saying what we don't do potentially helps alleviate any feelings that academic relationships and freedoms are eroded by 'homogenising' effects of workshops.

A possible future...?
Finally, imagine this scene. Stockholm. The Nobel Prize banquet. The laureate commences their acceptance speech: 'All this would have been impossible without that time management course I did years ago...'

Until this happens, there will be scepticism – and it's essential to our enterprises that we acknowledge its validity and deal with it appropriately.

Steve Hutchinson

Complementary ideas include **2, 7, 15** and **48**.

50 We have built it, why don't they come?

In 2009, the Postdoc Development Centre (PDC) at Imperial College London was launched. At the time it was the only standalone centre in the UK dedicated to the support and development of research staff and fellows. Imperial has 2,400 research staff and fellows, a highly successful Imperial College Research Fellowship scheme, a network of department research staff representatives, a cross-college committee, a series of events for fellows, and academic research staff champions in all the departments.

We are driven by a number of principles:

1) Being a postdoc is not a career;
2) Imperial does not want any member of research staff to leave the college unemployed unless they want to be;
3) Our programme is bespoke and tailored to what research staff need rather than what they want (i.e. a permanent academic job).

Research staff are able to take up to ten days' development opportunities a year (written in their contracts). Details of the programme can be found here: www.imperial.ac.uk/postdoc-development-centre/. The provision is excellent, with high feedback scores, full courses, and full waiting lists. Delivered across faculties and within individual departments, it is highly flexible and adaptable.

However, we still face challenges. Here I pose some questions with my reflections:

1. No research staff ever takes up their ten days' development a year – why not?

There is a view that ten days a year means ten full days' development a year. This is not our view. We believe that researchers should be much more creative in defining their development opportunities (e.g. being a member of a committee provides new skills and experience; taking part in public engagement activities or being a department representative)

2. Why don't more research staff take up the offer of reviewing draft job applications and participating in a mock interview?

Reviewing draft job applications and participating in a mock interview are 'just-in-time' activities. We believe that many researchers leave applying for a job to the last minute (don't we all?!), evidenced by the fact that we receive requests to review applications on the day of the deadline, and therefore there is no time to send it to someone to review. We think that the thought of having a mock interview is either too scary or viewed as unnecessary because 'my science will speak for itself'. Many of our researchers have never had such an interview, so we understand that it may feel intimidating. As for 'my science will speak for itself', we are aware that many researchers have never failed in academia, and this, coupled with a lack of awareness that the job market is extremely competitive, means that the value of having a mock interview is not understood.

3. Despite widespread and varied publicity, why do we still encounter research staff who have never heard of us?

In terms of publicity we do the following: website, Twitter, monthly newsletter, occasional emails, paper publicity, reps networks and academic champions, but our most effective publicity is 'word of mouth' and via department events. So we believe that people do not read the information which is sent out, don't make the link with the PDC, or simply do not take part in any department activities outside the lab.

4. Is there something missing in what we offer?

We are aware that much of our provision is 'front-loaded', i.e. for postdocs early in their career. This is because being a postdoc is not a career and people need to plan for that. We do, however, provide specific support for fellows (defined here as someone with a personal research award).

Conclusion

We have built it, why don't they come? Ensure what you provide is of the highest quality, put together a publicity strategy and don't be disheartened when take-up and engagement is low. It just takes time!

Liz Elvidge

Complementary ideas include **34** and **43**.

51 Collaborative working: a strategic alliance of two universities

The need to deliver a broad provision within modern doctorates and research contracts but with limited resources can present significant challenges to universities, regardless of their size and location. A possible solution may be realised through the economies of scale, the pooling of knowledge and talent, and the creative upwelling that may arise from institutional collaboration and strategic alliances.

In 2011, building on a history of successful collaborative activities, Aberystwyth and Bangor Universities (Wales, UK) announced a new strategic alliance. The alliance covers a broad range of university activities, including researcher development provision and funded doctoral training programmes, as well as shared approaches to achieving and maintaining HR Excellence in Research Awards, and in implementing the Concordat to Support the Career Development of Researchers.

Initiating the partnership
At the time of the alliance, both universities already had comprehensive doctoral training provisions, and were at a similar stage of expansion into broader researcher development practices. These similarities meant that shared programmes were applicable across both locations, and made it possible to identify courses suitable for joint delivery.

This researcher development collaboration was catalysed by the efforts of a small group of highly motivated individuals, and a more formal arrangement (such as a memorandum of understanding) will be developed to sustain the partnership long term, ensure continuity and resilience, and agree ownership of shared materials.

Collaborative benefits

We quickly realised a number of benefits from a collaborative programme:

- Maximising limited resources and avoiding duplication of effort;
- Different and fresh perspectives that broaden scope and content;
- Wider sharing of best practice improving programme quality;
- Participants network together (even via video conferencing) and can find potential research collaborators;
- Flexibility of recorded 'taught' sessions can also broaden coverage to those who are unable or unlikely to attend a training session face to face.

In addition, we quickly found that working across institutions also develops the researcher developers; and, when leading courses on collaboration, we can truly exemplify meaningful good practice.

On reflection – challenges and solutions

A key challenge in delivering joint courses is geographical separation, with indirect transport links. Externally funded provision can be held at venues halfway (reducing staff costs), and where funding is not available we use video conferencing technology (reducing preparation time, travel and venue costs). A co-facilitator at the remote site ensures a collegiate atmosphere.

While there are huge benefits to collaboration, it is also important to remember that there is a cost in terms of time to make agreements, set up logistics and agree content. This should not be overlooked.

Whilst a memorandum of understanding may help to ensure longevity beyond personnel changes and individual enthusiasm, ultimately trust between the collaborators is crucial, and it's important not to get hung up on issues of ownership of materials and ideas. As with all collaboration, people matter. As such, you need to find a collaborator at your partner institution who is enthusiastic, creative, open to new possibilities and likeminded with regard to ownership. Bear in mind that they may not necessarily be your opposite number, as was the case for us. Regardless of role, it is vital that you establish the needs and expectations of your partner.

Ultimately, with course materials, it is not the content but how it is delivered wherein the true value resides, therefore both parties should be open to sharing and learning from each other. Complementing and enhancing each other's approach is key, and it is important to build in space to reflect with the other party on the lessons from the collaboration. Starting with a small and discrete event to test the arrangements, expectations, relationships and boundaries of the collaboration – and then reflecting jointly upon the value to both parties – is certainly a sensible approach.

Collaborative futures
An ideal scenario for us would be that we were much closer geographical neighbours and could therefore increase the provision or even consider a single programme for both universities. But regardless, given that those Welsh miles will not get any shorter, our immediate aim is to ensure that all new researcher development provision will be jointly developed and jointly delivered.

Penny Dowdney and Gary Reed

Complementary ideas include **3**, **45** and **52**.

52 Crafting a high-value practitioner network

Engaging with a community of like-minded professionals enhances the working practices and repertoires of researcher developers. A 'high-value' network, with a clear common purpose and structured practices founded on the principles of andragogy, presents opportunities for career enhancement as well as practice development.

The need for a high-value network

Current views of higher education leadership position 'good leaders' as having influence and reputation locally within their own institution, and also across their sector or specialist field. This thinking can also be applied to leadership in researcher development. Colleagues can and often do contribute wider than their organisation to sharing and enhancing practice, and the channels of dissemination and feedback matter.

In response to national network changes, a tri-university development network was designed by representatives from three research-intensive universities in the UK. It was intended that a small group of individuals, representing universities with similar numbers of researchers, would engage in longitudinal practice development aligned with their institutional objectives. In doing so they would also grow their own professional repertoires and develop their careers.

The key philosophy of a high-value network: andragogy

Andragogy is the applied practice of teaching adult learners. Adults need to be *involved in the planning of their learning*. An adapted action learning set model can provide a time-bound, thematic, and longitudinal structure that is designed by all members and relevant to specific learning needs.

Adults *respond better to problem-centred than to content-oriented learning*. High value networks should have a forward focus, providing dedicated time to think critically and gain insight into projects that members wish to scope or progress. All members should have equal opportunity to receive support from the group, and a 'critical friend' coaching role can be adopted to enable insight for each member.

Adults learn best when there is *immediate relevance to their job*. Themes for each network event should be action-orientated to feed forward directly into practice, and time for real planning at institutional level factored in to the day plan. Developments and progress can be fed back into the group subsequently, bringing accountability to the group to take action in recognition of the time contribution of other network members.

Adults learn best when *experience provides the basis for learning activities*. A high value network membership will contain a range of individual expertise, across complementary areas of responsibility, and varied career backgrounds.

The membership makes the network high value

A small network will enable trust to develop between members and enable both good-quality working relationships and achievable outputs.

Select your participating institutions carefully; similar strategic priorities will help align the focus and context of the meetings. Contrasting governance, operational structures, and areas of expertise can help participants compare and evaluate approaches.

Recruiting members with a degree of autonomy in their work will help the group to use meeting time to make decisions, plan, and realise their next steps, having real impact back in the workplace.

Guest members with a particular expertise can be welcomed. Academic experts, for example in higher education policy, workplace learning and development, or doctoral pedagogy can help practitioners connect to relevant recent literatures.

Impact of the high-value network
Through our tri-university network, various achievements in addition to action learning and practice enhancement have been made, including:

- shared projects to map provision for doctoral supervisor development, engage with designing online learning, and enhance policy documents;
- establishing partner universities for multi-institution research studies;
- engaging with the researcher development scholarly literature in the form of a network journal club;
- designing and promoting reciprocal provision for distance learners who can access local support through university partnerships.

Kay Guccione and Sandy Sparks

Complementary ideas include **51** and **53**.

53 Academic credibility for researcher development

Increasing academic engagement and awareness of researcher development is crucial in gaining academic credibility. We have achieved this by reframing the context and language we use, articulating the evidence and impact we have against academic strategic priorities, and linking researcher development into academic development processes. These approaches have been key to our success in developing our own academic careers.

Our journey
Over the last ten years we have moved from employment as programme administrators to academics heading a Centre for Academic and Researcher Development.

How did we get here?
Key to our success has been the passion and belief that we make a difference for researchers. Having research backgrounds has enabled strong empathy and credibility with our audience. Our understanding of the importance of being strategic meant we reported the impact of our development programmes and alignment to institutional priorities to our senior leaders.

Steps in the process
We needed to up-skill and redefine our expertise in order to become proficient teachers. Training qualifications were initially very helpful for programme delivery, but academics understand the word 'teach' rather than 'train'. Subsequently we gained Senior Fellowships of the Higher Education Academy (www.heacademy. ac.uk) and changed the terminology we use around our work to talk about teaching rather than training.

Transitioning to academics

Traditionally, researcher developers support early career researchers. As the quality of our programmes was recognised, we were asked to expand delivery to academics and cover the full spectrum of academic activity – research excellence, inspirational teaching and professional development. This opportunity broadened our expertise, enabling interactions with external accrediting bodies, reporting to academic committees, and leading assessment and feedback. Our job descriptions then aligned most closely with our teaching-focused academic colleagues, and with the support of senior academic champions we were re-graded onto the academic scale. The Vice Dean for Teaching and Learning was particularly supportive as she understood the potential in us, rather than the job roles we held.

Developing the Centre

Being 'academics' gave access to new networks and committees and enabled us to see what is strategically important. Our performance targets and promotion criteria prioritise academic esteem indicators including grant income generation, scholarship and consultancy. We have taken opportunities to develop a national profile and influence the UK researcher development agenda and have translated our researcher development programmes internationally. We provide consultancy to institutions, charities and other funders of research. We have also expanded internal training programmes providing a continuum of support across academic career trajectories.

Mentors and champions

Key people have advised, supported and challenged our progress. To overcome challenges we have provided evidence that demonstrates the impact of our work. We recommend utilising multiple mentors from academic and professional service backgrounds within and outside the institution who can help you to think strategically.

Ownership and responsibility

It has been important for us to take the initiative and drive forward innovations. Don't be frustrated if the reaction from senior leaders is negative at first. Use language and terminology that will resonate with them and consider how your ambitions link into their wider responsibilities.

Saying yes to opportunities
In the short term, saying yes to opportunities has been beneficial for us, but be wary of over-committing. You are only as good as your last set of evaluation data. When saying yes, it is important to consider the resources required and staffing implications, as well as previous commitments.

Career development
We are committed to lifelong learning and actively seek opportunities to enhance our expertise, using our networks to work collaboratively. Moving onto the academic career ladder has enabled career progression within the role of researcher development and we both have successfully been further promoted using evidence and impact from our training programmes.

Judith Williams and Rachel Cowen

Complementary ideas include **5, 7, 9, 15** and **52**.

Appendix
Who are the researcher developers?: a UK survey

Researcher developers are a diverse group and the role varies considerably between universities. In spring 2015 we ran a UK-wide survey to find out more. Over 100 researcher developers responded and this is what they told us...

Most striking is that two-thirds have a PhD (compared to half of academic staff), making it a highly-qualified profession. The discipline background varies, with half coming from the sciences and a quarter each from the social sciences and the arts and humanities. Three-quarters are classified by their university as non-academic, but researcher developers are better described as 'blended professionals' – neither fully professional service (like finance or HR) nor fully academic, but containing elements of both. Notably, some institutions are beginning to recognise the dual nature of this and many similar roles in a modern university and are creating new classifications between 'academic' and 'professional services'.

Researcher developers are most commonly based either in a graduate school (27 per cent) or in HR (28 per cent). Being based in a graduate school can be challenging for those who work with research staff, who don't think to look to a graduate school for development opportunities. Similarly, being based in HR can be challenging for those working with research students.

What do researcher developers do – and how do they think others see them?
Respondents reported offering a wide range of activities supporting the development of researchers, but believed that

they were seen as offering a more limited range. In particular, researcher developers felt that they were underappreciated with a lack of recognition of their qualifications and a sense that they were seen as 'peddling soft skills'. Researcher developers stressed the importance of effective communication in telling colleagues across the institution what it is they actually do and its importance.

Researcher developer prerequisites and progression
With a research background prevalent, it is not surprising that half of researcher developers considered research experience or a PhD essential to their role, both in understanding their audience and in providing credibility. Knowledge of the HE landscape, teaching skills and passion for the role were also considered important. Many had gained or were working towards professional qualifications, the most popular of which were coaching, teaching and CIPD (Chartered Institute of Personnel and Development) accreditation and 70 per cent maintained a formal record of their development (compared to 56 per cent of respondents in an equivalent national survey of research staff). Despite their roles involving supporting researchers in developing a career development plan, only 46 per cent of researcher developers had a career development plan (compared to 52 per cent of research staff), providing a challenge to us to model the practices we advocate for researchers. Many noted that there was no clear career progression for them, and so many were unsure of their career aspirations with the most common aspiration being an increase in seniority, followed by freelance work, creating an academic classification for their role, and leaving HE.

Values of researcher developers
There is a clear vocational element in why researcher developers do their jobs, with respondents valuing development, wanting to support others to achieve their potential, and to improve the situation of future researchers. The variety and freedom within the role was noted positively, giving the impression of a bright and creative population who value their independence. These values are similar to those of senior academics whose roles contain substantial enabling activities and mentoring.

Similarities and differences with researchers

With so many researcher developers having a research background, how do the two populations compare in the UK? Similarities in concerns about career progression and in values held have already been noted. Notable differences include that researchers are typically on fixed-term contracts, but 90 per cent of researcher developers have open-ended contracts. Researcher developers are overwhelmingly British (90 per cent); 77 per cent have only worked in one institution as a researcher developer, compared to the more diverse and mobile researcher population, and researcher developers are more satisfied with their work–life balance (74 per cent compared to 69 per cent of research staff and 46 per cent of research leaders).

So what can we conclude?

Researcher developers belong to an enthusiastic, emerging profession and are keen to develop themselves as well as others. They typically enjoy freedom in their role, but consequently can feel ignored or misunderstood. There is an ongoing challenge of career planning and unclear career progression, which the sector is beginning to address with various initiatives (e.g. in the UK, the Vitae Career Framework for Researcher Developers – www. vitae.ac.uk/cfrd). Despite clear differences between researcher developers and their audiences, there are also strong similarities in the values that drive them.

Anna Price and Richard Freeman

Notes on contributors

Stuart Boon is the Academic Development Director within the University of Strathclyde's Organisational and Staff Development Unit and oversees and contributes to all accredited and non-accredited provision for researcher development, academic practice, and knowledge exchange.

Anne Boultwood (Birmingham City University) has considerable experience of researcher development and research-led public engagement. She established the Researcher Education and Development (RED) initiative to introduce a range of programmes and resources, and has led a number of them, including the AHRC-funded Knowledge Exchange in Design project.

Tony Bromley is a University of Leeds Senior Training and Development Officer, responsible for the Graduate Training and Support Centre and has worked in researcher development since 2002. He was lead author of the UK researcher development sector impact evaluation framework.

Billy Bryan is a PhD student in Medical Education (Sheffield), investigating the impact of specialised feedback methods on clinical learning strategies. He is also involved in research exploring the learning and life experiences of doctoral students.

Matthew Cheeseman is a writer and teacher. He runs the small press Spirit Duplicator, which is named after the machines that pre-dated photocopiers and printed in a purple, cucumber-smelling ink.

Laura Christie directs the Researcher Development Programme for doctoral students at Royal Holloway, University of London. She has over seven years' experience of teaching at HE level. Laura advises doctoral students with their thesis writing and designs and delivers the academic writing series.

Emma Compton-Daw is the Academic Development Lead for Research at Strathclyde University, providing leadership for the researcher development pathways. While a postdoctoral researcher, Emma has also been a chair of departmental and national research staff associations.

Fiona Conway is Academic Development Lead (Knowledge Exchange) at Strathclyde University. She designed and leads the Knowledge Exchange Development Pathway on the accredited programme and provides leadership for CPD development provision in the area.

Rachel Cowen is a Senior Lecturer and Researcher Development Consultant leading on research, teaching and personal and professional development programmes for research staff and academic staff at the University of Manchester. Rachel is also a qualified executive coach and a Senior Fellow of the Higher Education Academy (HEA).

Nicola Cuthbert is the Researcher Development and Enterprise Manager at the Institute for Academic Development (IAD) at The University of Edinburgh, where she manages the professional and personal development training and support offered by the IAD for research-active staff.

Rob Daley is an academic developer at Heriot-Watt University. His role includes researcher development, teaching development and quality assurance activities. He chairs the UKCGE (UK Council for Graduate Education) Postgraduate Student Experience Working Group and is a UK reviewer for the HR Excellence in Research award.

Fiona Denney is the Director of the Brunel Educational Excellence Centre at Brunel University London. Fiona has worked in UK universities for 20 years – as an academic and a researcher and staff developer, most notably at King's College London, prior to moving to Brunel in 2014.

Penny Dowdney is the Doctoral School Manager at Bangor University and KESS (Knowledge Economy Skills Scholarships) Wales Director. She works on training and development from PhD via early career researcher and through to doctoral supervisor within Bangor University, and in collaboration with all eight universities in Wales.

Nigel Eady is Head of Researcher Training and Development at King's College London. His teams deliver personal, professional and career development opportunities for doctoral researchers and research staff. A former biochemist, his goal is helping people achieve their potential.

Liz Elvidge is the head of the Postdoc Development Centre at Imperial College London. She is responsible for providing training and development opportunities for the College's 2,400 postdocs and fellows.

Dave Filipović-Carter runs Education-Training Ltd, which provides bespoke research(er) training. Particular areas of interest include the doctoral process, including supervision, and general topics on cultural difference. Dave is also an Associate Lecturer in Law at the Open University.

Richard Freeman is the Programme Leader for Researcher Development, Programme Leader for the Online MPhil/PhD and Deputy Director of the Bloomsbury Economic and Social Research Council (ESRC) Doctoral Training Centre at the Centre for Doctoral Education at University College London (UCL) Institute of Education, London.

Kay Guccione works at the University of Sheffield, where she specialises in evidence-led design of mentoring and coaching services for researchers. She investigates different aspects of the research experience and uses the findings to create partnerships that help people talk about the things that matter most to them.

Steve Hutchinson (www.hutchinsontraining.com) is a consultant, coach, trainer and author. He has been at the forefront of academic and researcher development for fifteen years and works internationally with a range of clients. His company specialises in leadership, communication and personal impact.

David Hyatt is a lecturer in Education at the University of Sheffield. He directs two doctoral (EdD) programmes and one master's (MEd). His current research interests are in HE pedagogy and policy. He is a Senior Fellow of the Higher Education Academy and holds a Senate Award for Sustained Excellence in Learning and Teaching.

Hilary Jones has a remit at the University of Sheffield to increase the number of postgraduate internships taking place across the institution. She manages the flagship Postgraduate Advantage internship scheme as well as acting in an advisory capacity to staff and students.

Hugh Kearns is recognised internationally as a public speaker, educator and researcher. He regularly lectures at universities across the world on the psychology of high performance, particularly relating to academia and research. He is based in Adelaide, Australia.

Helen Lawrence is an independent consultant and coach who works in a variety of organisations, helping individuals to be both more effective and aware of their values. She is based in East Yorkshire.

Lucy Lee is a researcher development manager at the University of Sheffield. She used a research-informed approach to create and develop the flagship researcher development programme in Sheffield which later became Think Ahead. Her expertise lies in whole-programme development and impact evaluation.

Heather McGregor is a learning and development professional who (at the time of writing) leads the Researcher Development Programme at Queen's University, Belfast. She has worked for 15 years in management and leadership development in three of the leading charities in the UK: British Heart Foundation; Cancer Research UK; and Save the Children.

Rhian Melita Morris is the Impact and Engagement Officer for the College of Science at Swansea University. She supports the development of researchers in three ways: providing training and guidance; providing opportunities to network and collaborate; and supporting external collaboration via public, business and social-media engagement.

Peter Matanle is Senior Lecturer and Director of Research and Innovation at the University of Sheffield's School of East Asian Studies. Recently he has taken an interest in developing an evidenced-based analysis of career progression among academics, with a view to identifying and resolving barriers to progression through mentoring and knowledge sharing.

Inger Mewburn has been specialising in research education since 2006. She is currently the Director of Research Training at The Australian National University, where she runs a small team of researcher developers and does research on student experience to inform practice.

Robert Myles is an actor, writer and filmmaker who graduated from the University of Leicester with a BSc in Psychology. He is committed to storytelling in all its forms, including freelance copywriting, performing Shakespeare, and producing bespoke video content.

Fehmidah Munir is a Reader in Health Psychology in the School of Sport, Exercise and Health Sciences at Loughborough University. She plays an active part in driving the Athena SWAN (www.ecu.ac.uk/equality-charters/athena-swan/) activities of the School and in developing her colleagues through training, mentoring and sponsorship.

Nicola Phillips is a Lecturer in Chemical Science at Manchester Metropolitan University. Alongside her research and teaching, Nicola advises and develops employability resources to help students and researchers.

Bryony Portsmouth is currently the Researcher Professional Development Team Leader at the University of Sheffield. With a background in careers guidance, people development and service improvement, Bryony has been working in HE for three and a half years. She is passionate about enhancing researcher development through sustainable organisational change.

Anna Price is Head of Researcher Development at Queen Mary University of London, where she leads a team who support the University's researchers to excel at their roles and develop their careers. Anna is also active in local, national and international networks.

Mark Proctor is the Academic Development Officer for Research at the University of Sunderland. He has enjoyed leading on the design, delivery and evaluation of postgraduate research student and research staff (including supervisor accreditation) development programmes for the last eight years.

Gary Reed is the Director of Research, Business & Innovation at Aberystwyth University, and works to enhance researcher development in conjunction with Bangor University. He chairs the HR Excellence in Research initiative for Aberystwyth, and is the University's Welsh Crucible Champion. In addition, he was seconded to the Leadership Foundation for HE as Assistant Director, Membership (Wales).

Heather Sears is a researcher developer at Coventry University, building on eleven years at the University of Leeds. She completed a PhD in microbiology and five years' postdoctoral research. Heather is passionate about developing bespoke cohort programmes for researchers.

Sara Shinton (https://iad4researchers.wordpress.com/) is Head of Researcher Development at The University of Edinburgh. She has almost 20 years' experience in researcher and academic development, with particular interests in collaboration, impact, resilience and funding.

Sandrine Soubes is the researcher development manager for the Faculty of Science at the University of Sheffield. Sandrine has a background in biological research, has worked on two different continents, and is now crossing her disciplinary anchor by studying higher education.

Sandy Sparks is the Learning & Development (L&D) Consultant for Research Staff at the University of Warwick. Sandy has UK and international experience, in private and public sectors, with HE experience since 1994. Sandy also facilitates, mediates and consults freelance on a wide range of HR and L&D areas.

Paul Spencer is the Researcher Development Manager at UWE Bristol (University of the West of England). He coordinates and delivers a programme of development opportunities for postgraduate researchers and research staff in conjunction with lots of brilliant people inside and outside of the university.

Richard Ward is a Research Associate in History at the University of Sheffield, working on a major research project, The Digital Panopticon: The Global Impact of London Punishments, 1780–1925. Prior to this he was a Research Fellow at the University of Leicester.

Jerry Wellington is a Professor in the School of Education at the University of Sheffield. He has a background in science and science education, although his current interests also lie in the fields of research methods, new issues in doctoral education and the development of postgraduate and new researchers.

Neil Willey is the Director of the Graduate School at University of the West of England, Bristol, and is responsible for championing the institution's strategic approach to postgraduate research study. He is also the module leader for the Research in Contemporary Context module.

Janet Wilkinson has a particular interest in developing women academics at all levels, and has worked in researcher development for the last 15 years as an independent researcher developer, based in the south-west of England.

Judith Williams is a highly regarded professor and teacher, having received the University of Manchester Teaching Excellence Award, a Distinguished Achievement Medal for Teacher of the Year and a Senior Fellowship from the Higher Education Academy.